MTTC 94 Integrated Science (Secondary)

Teacher Certification Exam

By: Sharon Wynne, M.S
Southern Connecticut State University

"And, while there's no reason yet to panic, I think it's only prudent that we make preparations to panic."

XAMonline, INC.

Boston

To obtain permission(s) to use the material from this work for any purpose including workshops or seminars, please submit a written request to:

XAMonline, Inc.
21 Orient Ave.
Melrose, MA 02176
Toll Free 1-800-509-4128
Email: info@xamonline.com
Web www.xamonline.com
Fax: 1-781-662-9268

Library of Congress Cataloging-in-Publication Data

Wynne, Sharon A.
    Integrated Science (Secondary) 94: Teacher Certification / Sharon A. Wynne. -2nd ed.
    ISBN 978-1-58197-972-5
        1. Integrated Science (Secondary) 94   2. Study Guides.   3. MTTC
        4. Teachers' Certification & Licensure.   5. Careers

Disclaimer:
The opinions expressed in this publication are the sole works of XAMonline and were created independently from the National Education Association, Educational Testing Service, or any State Department of Education, National Evaluation Systems or other testing affiliates.

Between the time of publication and printing, state specific standards as well as testing formats and website information may change that is not included in part or in whole within this product. Sample test questions are developed by XAMonline and reflect similar content as on real tests; however, they are not former tests. XAMonline assembles content that aligns with state standards but makes no claims nor guarantees teacher candidates a passing score. Numerical scores are determined by testing companies such as NES or ETS and then are compared with individual state standards. A passing score varies from state to state.

Printed in the United States of America   œ-1

MTTC: Integrated Science (Secondary) 94
ISBN: 978-1-58197-972-5

Table of Contents

Great Study and Testing Tips!

What to study in order to prepare for the subject assessments is the focus of this study guide but equally important is *how* you study.

You can increase your chances of truly mastering the information by taking some simple, but effective steps.

Study Tips:

1. <u>**Some foods aid the learning process**</u>. Foods such as milk, nuts, seeds, rice, and oats help your study efforts by releasing natural memory enhancers called CCKs (*cholecystokinin*) composed of *tryptopha*n, *choline*, and *phenylalanine*. All of these chemicals enhance the neurotransmitters associated with memory. Before studying, try a light, protein-rich meal of eggs, turkey, and fish. All of these foods release the memory enhancing chemicals. The better the connections, the more you comprehend.

Likewise, before you take a test, stick to a light snack of energy boosting and relaxing foods. A glass of milk, a piece of fruit, or some peanuts all release various memory-boosting chemicals and help you to relax and focus on the subject at hand.

2. <u>**Learn to take great notes**</u>. A by-product of our modern culture is that we have grown accustomed to getting our information in short doses (i.e. TV news sound bites or USA Today style newspaper articles.)

Consequently, we've subconsciously trained ourselves to assimilate information better in <u>neat little packages</u>. If your notes are scrawled all over the paper, it fragments the flow of the information. Strive for clarity. Newspapers use a standard format to achieve clarity. Your notes can be much clearer through use of proper formatting. A very effective format is called the *"Cornell Method."*

> Take a sheet of loose-leaf lined notebook paper and draw a line all the way down the paper about 1-2" from the left-hand edge.

> Draw another line across the width of the paper about 1-2" up from the bottom. Repeat this process on the reverse side of the page.

Look at the highly effective result. You have ample room for notes, a left hand margin for special emphasis items or inserting supplementary data from the textbook, a large area at the bottom for a brief summary, and a little rectangular space for just about anything you want.

3. Get the concept then the details. Too often we focus on the details and don't gather an understanding of the concept. However, if you simply memorize only dates, places, or names, you may well miss the whole point of the subject.

A key way to understand things is to put them in your own words. If you are working from a textbook, automatically summarize each paragraph in your mind. If you are outlining text, don't simply copy the author's words.

Rephrase them in your own words. You remember your own thoughts and words much better than someone else's, and subconsciously tend to associate the important details to the core concepts.

4. Ask Why? Pull apart written material paragraph by paragraph and don't forget the captions under the illustrations.

Example: If the heading is "Stream Erosion", flip it around to read "Why do streams erode?" Then answer the questions.

If you train your mind to think in a series of questions and answers, not only will you learn more, but it also helps to lessen the test anxiety because you are used to answering questions.

5. Read for reinforcement and future needs. Even if you only have 10 minutes, put your notes or a book in your hand. Your mind is similar to a computer; you have to input data in order to have it processed. *By reading, you are creating the neural connections for future retrieval.* The more times you read something, the more you reinforce the learning of ideas.

Even if you don't fully understand something on the first pass, *your mind stores much of the material for later recall.*

6. Relax to learn so go into exile. Our bodies respond to an inner clock called biorhythms. Burning the midnight oil works well for some people, but not everyone.

If possible, set aside a particular place to study that is free of distractions. Shut off the television, cell phone, pager and exile your friends and family during your study period.

If you really are bothered by silence, try background music. Light classical music at a low volume has been shown to aid in concentration over other types. Music that evokes pleasant emotions without lyrics are highly suggested. Try just about anything by Mozart. It relaxes you.

7. <u>**Use arrows not highlighters**</u>. At best, it's difficult to read a page full of yellow, pink, blue, and green streaks. Try staring at a neon sign for a while and you'll soon see that the horde of colors obscure the message.

A quick note, a brief dash of color, an underline, and an arrow pointing to a particular passage is much clearer than a horde of highlighted words.

8. <u>**Budget your study time**</u>. Although you shouldn't ignore any of the material, *allocate your available study time in the same ratio that topics may appear on the test.*

Testing Tips:

1. <u>Get smart, play dumb</u>. Don't read anything into the question. Don't make an assumption that the test writer is looking for something else than what is asked. Stick to the question as written and don't read extra things into it.

2. <u>Read the question and all the choices *twice* before answering the question</u>. You may miss something by not carefully reading, and then re-reading both the question and the answers.

If you really don't have a clue as to the right answer, leave it blank on the first time through. Go on to the other questions, as they may provide a clue as to how to answer the skipped questions.

If later on, you still can't answer the skipped ones . . . *Guess.* The only penalty for guessing is that you *might* get it wrong. Only one thing is certain; if you don't put anything down, you will get it wrong!

3. <u>Turn the question into a statement</u>. Look at the way the questions are worded. The syntax of the question usually provides a clue. Does it seem more familiar as a statement rather than as a question? Does it sound strange?

By turning a question into a statement, you may be able to spot if an answer sounds right, and it may also trigger memories of material you have read.

4. <u>Look for hidden clues</u>. It's actually very difficult to compose multiple-foil (choice) questions without giving away part of the answer in the options presented.

In most multiple-choice questions you can often readily eliminate one or two of the potential answers. This leaves you with only two real possibilities and automatically your odds go to Fifty-Fifty for very little work.

5. <u>Trust your instincts</u>. For every fact that you have read, you subconsciously retain something of that knowledge. On questions that you aren't really certain about, go with your basic instincts. **Your first impression on how to answer a question is usually correct.**

6. <u>Mark your answers directly on the test booklet</u>. Don't bother trying to fill in the optical scan sheet on the first pass through the test.

Just be very careful not to miss-mark your answers when you eventually transcribe them to the scan sheet.

7. <u>Watch the clock</u>! You have a set amount of time to answer the questions. Don't get bogged down trying to answer a single question at the expense of 10 questions you can more readily answer.

COMPETENCY 1.0 CONSTRUCTING NEW SCIENTIFIC KNOWLEDGE

Skill 1.1 Identify and apply procedures for gathering, organizing, interpreting, evaluating, and communicating data

Science may be defined as a body of knowledge that is systematically derived from study, observations and experimentation. Its goal is to identify and establish principles and theories that may be applied to solve problems. Pseudoscience, on the other hand, is a belief that is not warranted. There is no scientific methodology or application. Some of the more classic examples of pseudoscience include witchcraft, alien encounters, or any topics that are explained by hearsay.

The scientific method is the basic process behind science. It involves several steps from formulating a hypothesis to the conclusion.

Posing a question
Although many discoveries happen by chance the standard thought process of a scientist begins with forming a question to research. The more limited the question, the easier it is to set up an experiment to answer it.

Form a hypothesis
Once the question is formulated take an educated guess about the answer to the problem or question.

Conducting the test
To make a test fair data from an experiment must have a **variable** or any condition that can be changed such as temperature or mass. A good test will try to manipulate as few variables as possible so as to see which variable is responsible for the result. This requires a second example of a **control**. A control is an extra setup in which all the conditions are the same except for the variable being tested.

Observe and record the data
Reporting of the data should state specifics of how the measurements were calculated. A graduated cylinder needs to be read with proper procedures. As beginning students, technique must be part of the instructional process so as to give validity to the data.

Drawing a conclusion
After you record your data you compare it with that from the other groups. A conclusion is the judgment derived from the data results.

Graphing data

Graphing utilizes numbers to demonstrate patterns. The patterns offer a visual representation, making it easier to draw conclusions. The type of graphic representation used to display observations depends on the data that is collected. **Line graphs** are used to compare different sets of related data or to predict data that has not yet be measured. An example of a line graph would be comparing the rate of activity of different enzymes at varying temperatures. A **bar graph** or **histogram** is used to compare different items and make comparisons based on this data. An example of a bar graph would be comparing the ages of children in a classroom. A **pie chart** is useful when organizing data as part of a whole. A good use for a pie chart would be displaying the percent of time students spend on various after school activities.

As noted before, the independent variable is controlled by the experimenter. This variable is placed on the x-axis (horizontal axis). The dependent variable is influenced by the independent variable and is placed on the y-axis (vertical axis). It is important to choose the appropriate units for labeling the axes. It is best to take the largest value to be plotted and divide it by the number of block, and rounding to the nearest whole number.

Careful research and statistically significant figures will be your best allies should you need to defend your work. For this reason, make sure to use controls, work in a systematic fashion, keep clear records, and have reproducible results.

Descriptive Statistics

Modern science uses a number of disciplines to understand it better. Statistics is one of those subjects, which is absolutely essential for science.

Mean: Mean is the mathematical average of all the items. To calculate the mean, all the items must be added up and divided by the number of items. This is also called the arithmetic mean or more commonly as the "average".

Median: The median depends on whether the number of items is odd or even. If the number is odd, then the median is the value of the item in the middle. This is the value that denotes that the number of items having higher or equal value to that is same as the number of items having equal or lesser value than that. If the number of the items is even, the median is the average of the two items in the middle, such that the number of items having values higher or equal to it is same as the number of items having values equal or less than that.

Mode: Mode is the value of the item that occurs the most often if there are not many items. Bimodal is a situation where there are two items with equal frequency.

Range: Range is the difference between the maximum and minimum values. The range is the difference between two extreme points on the distribution curve.

Analysis of data to identify limitations, make predictions, and draw conclusions

Once data has been collected and organized, we can begin to interpret the findings. First, the uncertainly inherent in the data must be considered. Most scientists try to limit uncertainly by making repeated measurements. But there is typically variability between these measurements, which leads to further uncertainty. Statistics are typically performed on the data to help an investigator determine how confident he should be with the results. Such statistics can also help to determine whether differences between groups are "statistically significant". At this point, a scientist may chose to repeat certain experiments. This is expected, given that the scientific process is iterative. However, there will always be uncertainty that places a limitation on interpreting the results.

Next, the results will be examined to determine whether they support or disprove the original hypothesis. If the experiments were designed to properly test the hypothesis, they should at least be able to provide disproof or support. However, they may also show that more experiments are needed to clarify phenomena. Any useful hypothesis should allow the formation of predictions. Logical and deductive reasoning typically need to be combined with the hypothesis to do so effectively. Predictions may encompass the outcome of a laboratory experiment or of natural phenomena. Predictions can also be statistical and deal only with probabilities.

Science is limited by the available technology. An example of this would be the relationship of the discovery of the cell and the invention of the microscope. As our technology improves, more hypotheses will become theories and possibly laws. Science is also limited by the data that is able to be collected. Data may be interpreted differently on different occasions. Science limitations cause explanations to be changeable as new technologies emerge. Scientific theory and experimentation must be repeatable. It is also possible to be disproved and is capable of change. Science depends on communication, agreement, and disagreement among scientists.

Skill 1.2   Identify and apply principles and procedures of research and experimental design

An experiment is proposed and performed with the sole objective of testing a hypothesis. When evaluating an experiment, it is important to first look at the question it was supposed to answer. How logically did the experiment flow from there? How many variables existed? (it is best to only test one variable at a time)

You discover a scientist conducting an experiment with the following characteristics. He has two rows each set up with four stations. The first row has a piece of tile as the base at each station. The second row has a piece of linoleum as the base at each station. The scientist has eight eggs and is prepared to drop one over each station. What is he testing? He is trying to answer whether or not the egg is more likely to break when dropped over one material as opposed to the other material. His hypothesis might have been: The egg will be less likely to break when dropped over linoleum. This is a simple experiment. If the experiment was more complicated, or for example, conducted on a microscopic level, one might want to examine the appropriateness of the instruments utilized and their calibration.

Sampling

In cases where the number of events or individuals is too large to collect data on each one, scientists collect information from only a small percentage. This is known as sampling. If sampling is done correctly, it should give the investigator nearly the same information he would have obtained by testing the entire population. There are a variety of sampling techniques; random, systematic, stratified, cluster, and quota are just a few. While random sampling is typically the "gold standard", sometimes compromises must be made to save time, money, or effort.

Another important consideration in sampling is sample size. Again, a large sample will yield the most accurate information, but other factors often limit sample size. Statistical methods may be used to determine how large a sample is necessary to give an investigator a specified level of certainty (95% is a typical confidence interval). Conversely, if a scientist has a sample of certain size, those same statistical methods can be used to determine how confident the scientist can be that the sample accurately reflects the whole population.

Sampling can be collecting pieces/specimens or making instrument data points/observations at determined intervals or areas for the purpose of research/investigation. Sampling includes animal tracking, capturing, plant and animal tagging, plot sampling, specimen collecting, transect sampling, water sampling etc. The results obtained are used as representative of the whole research area or population.

Lab Report

Normally, knowledge is integrated in the form of a lab report. It should include a specific title and tell exactly what is being studied. The abstract is a summary of the report written at the beginning of the paper. The purpose should always be defined and will state the problem. The purpose should include the hypothesis (educated guess) of what is expected from the outcome of the experiment. The entire experiment should relate to this problem. It is important to describe exactly what was done to prove or disprove a hypothesis. Only one **variable** should be manipulated at one time. The variable you are adjusting is called the experimental, or manipulated, variable. What remains unchanged is the control. A **control** is necessary to prove that the results occurred from the changed conditions and would not just happen normally. Observations and results of the experiment should be recorded including all results from data. Drawings, graphs and illustrations should be included to support information. Observations are objective, whereas analysis and interpretation is subjective. A conclusion should explain why the results of the experiment either proved or disproved the hypothesis.

A scientific theory is an explanation of a set of related observations based on a proven hypothesis. A scientific law usually lasts longer than a scientific theory and has more data to back it up.

Skill 1.3 Apply knowledge of methods and equipment used in measurement to solve problems

There is a specific instrument for measuring each type of matter. One would not use a ruler to measure liquid, nor a graduated cylinder to measure a cell. The most common instruments found in a school laboratory are the graduated cylinder, balance, and buret.

Graduated Cylinder - These are used for precise measurements. They should always be placed on a flat surface. The surface of the liquid will form a meniscus (a lens-shaped curve). The measurement is read at the bottom of this curve.

Balance - Electronic balances are easier to use, but more expensive. An electronic balance should always be tarred before measuring and used on a flat surface. Substances should always be placed on a piece of paper to avoid messes and damage to the instrument. Triple beam balances must be used on a level surface. There are screws located at the bottom of the balance to make any adjustments. Start with the largest counterweight first to the last notch that does not tip the balance. Do the same with the next largest, etc until the pointer remains at zero. The total mass is the total of all the readings on the beams. Again, use paper under the substance to protect the equipment.

Buret – A buret is used to dispense precisely measured volumes of liquid. A stopcock is used to control the volume of liquid being dispensed at a time.

Mathematics are used extensively in science. Following a measurement, students may be required to convert units or to solve for an unknown using algebra.

Skill 1.4   **Identify and apply the safe and proper use of tools, equipment, and materials (including chemicals and living organisms) related to classroom and other science investigations**

Safety in the science classroom and laboratory is of paramount importance to the science educator. The following is a general summary of the types of safety equipment that should be made available within a given school system as well as general locations where the protective equipment or devices should be maintained and used. Please note that this is only a partial list and that your school system should be reviewed for unique hazards and site-specific hazards at each facility.

Safety Equipment

- Keep appropriate safety equipment on hand, including an emergency shower, eye-wash station, fume hood, fire blankets, and fire extinguisher. All students and teacher(s) should have and wear safety goggles and protective aprons when working in the lab.

- Ensure proper eye protection devices are worn by everyone engaged in supervising, observing, or conducting science activities involving potential hazards to the eye.

- Provide protective rubber or latex gloves for students when they dissect laboratory specimens.

- Use heat-safety items such as safety tongs, mittens, and aprons when handling either cold or hot materials.

- Use safety shields or screens whenever there is potential danger that an explosion or implosion might occur.

- Keep a bucket of 90 percent sand and 10 percent vermiculite or kitty litter (dried bentonite particles) in all rooms in which chemicals are handled or stored. The bucket must be properly labeled and have a lid that prevents other debris from contaminating the contents.

Teaching Procedures

- Set a good example when demonstrating experiments by modeling safety techniques such as wearing aprons and goggles.

- Help students develop a positive attitude toward safety. Students should not fear doing experiments or using reagents or equipment, but they should respect them for potential hazards.

- Always demonstrate procedures before allowing students to begin the activity. Look for possible hazards and alert students to potential dangers.

- Explain and post safety instructions each time you do an experiment.

- Maintain constant supervision of student activities. Never allow students to perform unauthorized experiments or conduct experiments in the laboratory alone.

- Protect all laboratory animals and ensure that they are treated humanely.

- Remind students that many plants have poisonous parts and should be handled with care.

- For safety, consider the National Science Teachers Association's recommendation to limit science classes to 24 or fewer students.

Student Safety Tips

- Read lab materials in advance. Note all cautions (written and oral).

- Never assume an experiment is safe just because it is in print.

- Do not eat or drink in the laboratory.

- Keep personal items off the lab tables.

- Restrain long hair and loose clothing. Wear laboratory aprons when appropriate.

- Avoid all rough play and mischief in science classrooms or labs.

- Wear closed-toed shoes when conducting experiments with liquids or with heated or heavy items.

- Never use mouth suction when filling pipettes with chemical reagents.

- Never force glass tubing into rubber stoppers.

- Avoid transferring chemicals to your face, hands, or other areas of exposed skin.

- Thoroughly clean all work surfaces and equipment after each use.

- Make certain all hot plates and burners are turned off before leaving the laboratory.

Lab Environment

- Place smoke, carbon monoxide, and heat detectors in laboratories and storerooms.

- Ensure that all new laboratories have two unobstructed exits. Consider adding additional exits to rooms with only one door.

- Frequently inspect a laboratory's electrical, gas, and water systems.

- Install ground fault circuit interrupters at all electrical outlets in science laboratories.

- Install a single central shut-off for gas, electricity, and water for all the laboratories in the school, especially if your school is in an earthquake zone.

- Maintain Material Safety Data Sheets (MSDS) on all school chemicals and an inventory of all science equipment.

First Response Protocols

All students and staff should be trained in first aid in the science classroom and laboratory. Please remember to **always report all accidents, however minor, to the lab instructor immediately.** In most situations **911** should immediately be called. Please refer to your school's specific safety plan for accidents in the classroom and laboratory. The classroom/laboratory should have a complete first-aid kit with supplies that are up-to-date and checked frequently for expiration.

Know the location and use of fire extinguishers, eye-wash stations and safety showers in the lab.

Do not attempt to smother a fire in a beaker or flask with a fire extinguisher. The force of the stream of material from it will turn over the vessel and result in a bigger fire. Just place a watch glass or a wet towel over the container to cut off the supply of oxygen.

If your clothing is on fire, **do not run** because this only increases the burning. It is normally best to fall on the floor and roll over to smother the fire. If a student whose clothing is on fire panics and begins to run, attempt to get the student on the floor and roll over to smother the flame. If necessary, use the fire blanket or safety shower in the lab to smother the fire.

Students with long hair should put their hair in a bun or a ponytail to prevent their hair from catching on fire.

Below are common accidents that everyone who uses the laboratory should be trained in how to respond.

- **Burns (Chemical or Fire)** – Use deluge shower for 15 minutes.
- **Burns (Clothing on fire)** – Use safety shower *immediately*. Keep victim immersed 15 minutes to wash away both heat and chemicals. All burns should be examined by medical personnel.
- **Chemical spills** – Chemical spills on hands or arms should be washed immediately with soap and water. Washing hands should become an instinctive response to any chemical spilled on hands. Spills that cover clothing and other parts of the body should be drenched under the safety shower. If strong acids or bases are spilled on clothing, the clothing should be removed.
- If a large area is affected, remove clothing and immerse victim in the *safety shower*. If a small area is affected, remove article of clothing and use deluge shower for 15 minutes.
- **Eyes (chemical contamination)** – Hold the eye wide open and flush with water from the eye wash for about 15 minutes. Seek medical attention.
- **Ingestion of chemicals or poisoning** – See antidote chart on wall of lab for general first-aid directions. The victim should drink large amounts of water. All chemical poisonings should receive medical attention.

Specific Safety Tips

Safety glasses/goggles. Safety glasses or goggles should be used during all activities where chemicals or particles may accidentally enter the eye. Common settings include middle and high school science labs, art studios, maintenance and shop areas. Be sure to review and consider the types of hazards present when selecting appropriate eye protection. Make sure you select equipment that is designed to provide protection for the risks under consideration.

Gloves. Many chemicals can either damage the skin via contact or may cause harm if allowed to be absorbed through the skin. As a result, it is important to use protective gloves to form a barrier to prevent these problems. Also, remember that different hazards require the use of different gloves. It is rare that one type of glove would be capable of providing adequate protection for all the hazards that may be encountered. This is especially true with regard to the variety of chemicals that may be found in science laboratories. Common settings include middle and high school science labs, art studios, maintenance and shop areas.

Lab coats and aprons. Lab coats and aprons are designed to provide protection in the event of a spill. In addition, the use of these articles may prevent student or staff clothing from becoming contaminated and thereby limit the migration of chemical contamination should a spill occur. Common settings include middle and high school science labs, art studios, maintenance and shop areas.

Eye wash units. Eye wash units should be provided in all areas where chemical or physical hazards exist which may cause eye irritation or injury.

Deluge showers/fire blankets. Deluge showers and fire blankets should be maintained in all areas where chemical or fire hazards exist which may result in partial body exposure.

Fire extinguishers. Fire extinguishers should be maintained in accordance to state and local fire and building codes. Furthermore, each area should be reviewed individually to determine if additional fire protection is required. Also, be sure to verify that the correct size and type of extinguisher is provided in accordance to the materials commonly used or maintained in that space.

Ventilation. Additional mechanical ventilation such as chemical fume hoods should be provided in all areas where chemical fumes, vapors or odors are commonly generated. Sufficient ventilation should be provided to prevent the build up of hazardous air contaminants and to minimize nuisance odors. This may be an issue in middle and high school art, science and shop classrooms as well as facilities maintenance shops.

Respirators. Respirators are not generally recommended for student use, but their use by maintenance staff may be required when conducting certain activities such as pesticide application or asbestos management.

Hearing protection. Certain lab and maintenance activities may necessitate the need to wear hearing protection. Each school system is encouraged to investigate all activities which generate loud or persistent noises for evaluation by a trained certified industrial hygienist.

Spill kits. **Spills will occur!** Be prepared to address and respond to the problem. This approach will enhance your ability to remediate a spill and minimize its long-term impact.

Chemical storage cabinets. The bulk storage of hazardous materials may necessitate the use of a reinforced chemical storage cabinet. This method of storage is routinely used to manage flammables, corrosives and oxidizers. Review local fire prevention guidance for storage recommendations.

Use of organisms

Dissections - Animals which are not obtained from recognized sources should not be used. Decaying animals or those of unknown origin may harbor pathogens and/or parasites. Specimens should be rinsed before handling. Latex gloves are desirable. If gloves are not available, students with sores or scratches should be excused from the activity. Formaldehyde is a carcinogenic and should be avoided or disposed of according to district regulations. Students objecting to dissections for moral reasons should be given an alternative assignment.

Live specimens - No dissections may be performed on living mammalian vertebrates or birds. Lower order life and invertebrates may be used. Biological experiments may be done with all animals except mammalian vertebrates or birds. No physiological harm may result to the animal. All animals housed and cared for in the school must be handled in a safe and humane manner. Animals are not to remain on school premises during extended vacations unless adequate care is provided. Many state laws state that any instructor who intentionally refuses to comply with the laws may be suspended or dismissed.

Microbiology - Pathogenic organisms must never be used for experimentation. Students should adhere to the following rules at all times when working with microorganisms to avoid accidental contamination:

1. Treat all microorganisms as if they were pathogenic.
2. Maintain sterile conditions at all times

Laboratory Chemicals

All laboratory solutions should be prepared as directed in the lab manual. Care should be taken to avoid contamination. All glassware should be rinsed thoroughly with distilled water before using, and cleaned well after use. Safety goggles should be worn while working with glassware in case of an accident. All solutions should be made with distilled water as tap water contains dissolved particles which may affect the results of an experiment. Chemical storage should be located in a secured, dry area. Chemicals should be stored in accordance with reactability. Acids are to be locked in a separate area. Used solutions should be disposed of according to local disposal procedures. Any questions regarding safe disposal or chemical safety may be directed to the local fire department.

If you are taking a national level exam you should check the Department of Education for your state for safety procedures. You will want to know what your state expects of you not only for the test but also for performance in the classroom for the good welfare of your students and others.

COMPETENCY 2.0   REFLECTING ON SCIENTIFIC KNOWLEDGE

Skill 2.1   Analyze the historical development of major scientific ideas

The history of biology traces man's understanding of the living world from the earliest recorded history to modern times. Though the concept of biology as a field of science arose only in the 19th century, the origin of biological sciences could be traced back to ancient Greeks (Galen and Aristotle).

During the Renaissance and Age of Discovery, renewed interest in the rapidly increasing number of known organisms generated a lot of interest in biology.

Andreas Vesalius (1514-1564), a Belgian anatomist and physician whose dissections of the human body and descriptions of his findings helped to correct the misconceptions of science. The books Vesalius wrote on anatomy were the most accurate and comprehensive anatomical texts to date.

Anton van Leeuwenhoek is known as the father of microscopy. In the 1650's, Leeuwenhoek began making tiny lenses that gave magnifications up to 300x. He was the first to see and describe bacteria, yeast plants, and the microscopic life found in water. Over the years, light microscopes have advanced to produce greater clarity and magnification. The scanning electron microscope (SEM) was developed in the 1950's. Instead of light, a beam of electrons passes through the specimen. Scanning electron microscopes have a resolution about one thousand times greater than light microscopes. The disadvantage of the SEM is that the chemical and physical methods used to prepare the sample result in the death of the specimen.

Robert Hooke (1635-1703) was a renowned inventor, a natural philosopher, astronomer, experimenter and a cell biologist. He deserves more recognition than he has been given, but is remembered mainly for his law, the Hooke's law, an equation describing elasticity that is still used today. He was the type of scientist that was then called a "virtuoso", able to contribute findings of major importance in any field of science. Hooke published *Micrographia* in 1665. Hooke devised the compound microscope and illumination system, one of the best microscopes of his time, and used it in his demonstrations at the Royal Society's meetings. With it he observed organisms as diverse as insects, sponges, bryozoans, foraminifera, and bird feathers. Micrographia is an accurate and detailed record of his observations, illustrated with magnificent drawings.

Carl Von Linnaeus (1707-1778), a Swedish botanist, physician and zoologist is well known for his contributions in ecology and taxonomy. Linnaeus is famous for his binomial system of nomenclature in which each living organism has two names, a genus and a species name. He is considered as the father of modern ecology and taxonomy.

In the late 1800's, Pasteur discovered the role of microorganisms in the cause of disease, pasteurization, and the rabies vaccine. Koch took these observations one step further by formulating that specific diseases were caused by specific pathogens. **Koch's postulates** are still used as guidelines in the field of microbiology; the same pathogen must be found in every diseased person, the pathogen must be isolated and grown in culture, the disease is induced in experimental animals from the culture, and the same pathogen must be isolated from the experimental animal.

Mattias Schleiden, a German botanist is famous for his cell theory. He observed plant cells microscopically and concluded that the cell is the common structural unit of plants. He proposed the cell theory along with Schwann, a zoologist, who observed cells in animals.

In the 18th century, many fields of science like botany, zoology and geology began to evolve as scientific disciplines in the modern sense.

In the 20th century, the rediscovery of Mendel's work led to the rapid development of genetics by Thomas Hunt Morgan and his students.

DNA structure was another key event in biological study. In the 1950s, James Watson and Francis Crick discovered the structure of a DNA molecule as that of a double helix. This structure made it possible to explain DNA's ability to replicate and to control the synthesis of proteins.

Francois Jacob and Jacques Monod contributed greatly to the field of lysogeny and bacterial reproduction by conjugation and both of them won the Nobel Prize for their contributions.

Following the cracking of the genetic code, biology has largely split between organismal biology consisting of ecology, ethology, systematics, paleontology, evolutionary biology, developmental biology, and other disciplines that deal with whole organisms or groups of organisms and the disciplines related to molecular biology including cell biology, biophysics, biochemistry, neuroscience, immunology, and many other overlapping subjects.

The use of animals in biological research has expedited many scientific discoveries. Animal research has allowed scientists to learn more about animal biological systems, including the circulatory and reproductive systems. One significant use of animals is for the testing of drugs, vaccines, and other products (such as perfumes and shampoos) before use or consumption by humans. Along with the pros of animal research, the cons are also very significant. The debate about the ethical treatment of animals has been ongoing since the introduction of animals in research. Many people believe the use of animals in research is cruel and unnecessary. Animal use is federally and locally regulated. The purpose of the Institutional Animal Care and Use Committee (IACUC) is to oversee and evaluate all aspects of an institution's animal care and use program.

Skill 2.2   Recognize and describe interrelationships among the life, physical, and earth sciences and among science, mathematics, and technology

Biological science is closely connected to technology and the other sciences and greatly impacts society and everyday life. Scientific discoveries often lead to technological advances and, conversely, technology is often necessary for scientific investigation and advances in technology often expand the reach of scientific discoveries. In addition, biology and the other scientific disciplines share several unifying concepts and processes that help unify the study of science. Finally, because biology is the science of living systems, biology directly impacts society and everyday life.

Unifying concepts and processes among the sciences

The following are the concepts and processes generally recognized as common to all scientific disciplines:

- Systems, order, and organization

- Evidence, models, and explanation

- Constancy, change, and measurement

- Evolution and equilibrium

- Form and function

Systems, order, and organization

Because the natural world is so complex, the study of science involves the **organization** of items into smaller groups based on interaction or interdependence. These groups are called **systems**. Examples of organization are the periodic table of elements and the six-kingdom classification scheme for living organisms. Examples of systems are the solar system, cardiovascular system, Newton's laws of force and motion, and the laws of conservation.

Order refers to the behavior and measurability of organisms and events in nature. The arrangement of planets in the solar system and the life cycle of bacterial cells are examples of order.

Evidence, models, and explanations

Scientists use **evidence** and **models** to form **explanations** of natural events. Models are miniaturized representations of a larger event or system. Evidence is anything that furnishes proof.

Constancy, change, and measurement

Constancy and **change** describe the observable properties of natural organisms and events. Scientists use different systems of **measurement** to observe change and constancy. For example, the freezing and melting points of given substances and the speed of sound are constant under constant conditions. Growth, decay, and erosion are all examples of natural change.

Evolution and equilibrium

Evolution is the process of change over a long period of time. While biological evolution is the most common example, one can also classify technological advancement, changes in the universe, and changes in the environment as evolution.

Equilibrium is the state of balance between opposing forces of change. Homeostasis and ecological balance are examples of equilibrium.

Form and function

Form and **function** are properties of organisms and systems that are closely related. The function of an object usually dictates its form and the form of an object usually facilitates its function. For example, the form of the heart (e.g. muscle, valves) allows it to perform its function of circulating blood through the body.

Biological applications

Because biology is the study of living things, we can easily apply the knowledge of biology to daily life and personal decision making. For example, biology greatly influences the health decisions humans make everyday. What foods to eat, when and how to exercise, and how often to bathe are just three of the many decisions we make everyday that are based on our knowledge of biology. Other areas of daily life where biology affects decision making are parenting, interpersonal relationships, family planning and consumer spending.

Skill 2.3   Analyze the nature of scientific thought and inquiry

Science is Empirical, Verifiable, and Logical

Observations, however general they may seem, lead scientists to create a viable question and an educated guess (hypothesis) about what to expect. While scientists often have laboratories set up to study a specific thing, it is likely that along the way they will find an unexpected result. It is always important to be open-minded and to look at all of the information. An open-minded approach to science provides room for more questioning, and hence, more learning. A central concept in science is that all evidence is empirical. This means that all evidence must be observed by the five senses. The phenomenon must be both observable and measurable, with reproducible results.

The question stage of scientific inquiry involves repetition. By repeating the experiment you can discover whether or not you have reproducibility. If results are reproducible, the hypothesis is valid. If the results are not reproducible, one has more questions to ask. It is also important to recognize that one experiment is often a stepping-stone for another. It is possible that data will be retested (by the same scientist or by another), and that a different conclusion may be found. In this way, scientific competition acts as a system of checks and balances.

Evaluating Scientific claims

Because people often attempt to use scientific evidence in support of political or personal agendas, the ability to evaluate the credibility of scientific claims is a necessary skill in today's society. In evaluating scientific claims made in the media, public debates and advertising, one should follow several guidelines.

First, scientific, peer-reviewed journals are the most accepted source for information on scientific experiments and studies. One should carefully scrutinize any claim that does not reference peer-reviewed literature.

Second, the media and those with an agenda to advance (advertisers, debaters, etc.) often overemphasize the certainty and importance of experimental results. One should question any scientific claim that sounds fantastical or overly certain.

Finally, knowledge of experimental design and the scientific method is important in evaluating the credibility of studies. For example, one should look for the inclusion of control groups and the presence of data to support the given conclusions.

Bias

Scientific research can be biased in the choice of what data to consider, in the reporting or recording of the data, and/or in how the data are interpreted. The scientist's emphasis may be influenced by his/her nationality, sex, ethnic origin, age, or political convictions. For example, when studying a group of animals, male scientists may focus on the social behavior of the males and typically male characteristics.

Although bias related to the investigator, the sample, the method or the instrument may not be completely avoidable in every case, it is important to know the possible sources of bias and how bias could affect the evidence. Moreover, scientists need to be attentive to possible bias in their own work as well as that of other scientists.

Objectivity may not always be attained. However, one precaution that may be taken to guard against undetected bias is to have many different investigators or groups of investigators working on a project. By different, it is meant that the groups are made up of various nationalities, ethnic origins, ages, and political convictions and composed of both males and females. It is also important to note one's aspirations, and to make sure to be truthful to the data, even when grants, promotions, and notoriety are at risk.

Skill 2.4   Recognize and describe relationships among scientific discoveries, technological developments, and society

Science and technology

Science and technology, while distinct concepts, are closely related. Science attempts to investigate and explain the natural world, while technology attempts to solve human adaptation problems. Technology often results from the application of scientific discoveries, and advances in technology can increase the impact of scientific discoveries. For example, Watson and Crick used science to discover the structure of DNA and their discovery led to many biotechnological advances in the manipulation of DNA. These technological advances greatly influenced the medical and pharmaceutical fields. The success of Watson and Crick's experiments, however, was dependent on the technology available. Without the necessary technology, the experiments would have failed.

The combination of biology and technology has improved the human standard of living in many ways. However, the negative impact of increasing human life expectancy and population on the environment is problematic. In addition, advances in biotechnology (ie. genetic engineering, cloning) produce ethical dilemmas that society must consider.

Science and society

In the last century, the advances in the fields of science and technology were amazing and have changed the lives of human beings forever. Lifestyles were greatly affected and the society experienced dramatic changes. People started to take science and technology very seriously. The advances in these two interrelated fields are no longer the domain of the elite and sophisticated. The average person started to use the advances in the field of technology in their daily lives. Because of this, the societal structure is changing rapidly to the extent that even young children are using technology.

With any rapid change, there are always good and poor things associated with it. Caution and care are the two words we need to associate with these giant strides in technology. At the same time, we need high technology in our lives and we can't afford to not make use of these developments and reap the benefits for the good of humanity.

Our environment in which we live, human biology, society at large, and our culture are being affected.

Let us take each point and examine very carefully the effects of science and technology on the above.

1. Environment:

The environment we live in is constantly and rapidly undergoing tremendous changes. The positive effects include ability to predict hurricanes, measuring the changes in terms of radioactivity present in our environment, the remedial measures for that problem, predicting the levels of gases like carbon monoxide, carbon dioxide, and other harmful gases, various estimates like the greenhouse effect, ozone layer and UV radiation to name a few. With the help of modern technology, it is possible to know their quantities and to monitor and plan and implement measures to deal with them. Even with the most advanced technology available to us, it is impossible to go back to the clean, green earth, since man has made a mark on it in a negative way. It is possible to a limited extent to alleviate the problem, but it is impossible to eradicate it.

The negative aspects of the effect of technology on our environment are numerous. The first and foremost is pollution of various kinds - water, air, noise etc. The greenhouse effect, the indiscriminate use of fertilizers, the spraying of pesticides, the use of various additives to our food, deforestation, unprecedented exploitation of non renewable energy resources are just a few of these negative effects. As we discussed earlier, it is not possible to solve these problems with money or human resources, but educating the society and making them aware of these negative aspects will go a long way. For example, as teachers we need to educate students about using natural resources cautiously and ways to save those resources. We also need to teach that little steps in the right direction will go a long way ie., car pooling, not wasting paper and whenever possible, to walk (if it is safe). It is important to teach the students to value trees and other plants Since they return oxygen to the atmosphere.

2. Human biology:

The strides made by science and technology have lasting effects on human biology. A few examples are organ transplants, in vitro fertilization, cloning, new drugs, new understanding of various diseases, cosmetic surgery, reconstructive surgery, use of computers in operations, lasers in medicine and forensic science. These changes have made lasting differences to the humanity. As always there are pros and cons to these changes.

The obvious positive aspects are in medicine. People with organ transplants have renewed hope. Their life spans are increased and their quality of life has changed with the use of technology such as pacemakers. Couples who experienced infertility are having babies now. Corrective and cosmetic surgery are giving new confidence to patients. Glasses to correct vision problems are being replaced slowly by laser surgery.

The negative aspects include paternity issues arising out of in vitro fertilization and some medical blunders, which are expensive and heart wrenching (when a wrong egg is implanted), the indiscriminate use of corrective and cosmetic surgery, older mothers who die and leave young orphans.

3. Society:
Society is not the same as it used to be even twenty-five years ago. The use of technology has changed our patterns of lifestyle, our behavior, our ethical and moral thinking, our economy and career opportunities to name a few.

The positive effects are the booming economy due to the high tech industry, more career opportunities for people to select, raising of the standard of living, prolonged life with quality, closeness even though we are separated by thousands of kilometers/miles and quicker and faster communication. The computer has contributed a lot to these changes. Normal household chores are being done by machines, a cost effective and time saving means for upkeep of kitchen and home, giving relief to a busy lifestyle.

The negative aspects are far reaching. The breakdown in family structure could be attributed partly to advanced technology. Family meals and family togetherness are being replace with gadgets. Some would argue that as a result of this, our young people are becoming insecure which indirectly affects their problem solving skills. Young people are becoming increasingly vulnerable due to Internet programs including chat rooms and online pornography. There must be stringent measures to protect our younger generation from these Internet predators. The effects of various high tech gadgets like the microwave are not entirely positive. Constant video game playing utilizing new technology may encourage a sedentary lifestyle and increase childhood obesity.

4. Culture:
This is a very sensitive yet very important issue. Those above listed factors are affecting the culture of people.

The positive aspects are that technology is uniting us to a certain extent. For example, it is possible to communicate with a person of any culture without seeing them face to face. It makes business and personal communication much easier over long distances. Some people were not comfortable with communicating with other cultures since they were closed societies, but e-mail has changed that. When we all use the same pieces of technology a common ground is established. The Internet can definitely boast of some successful cross-cultural marriages. Sharing opinions and information has been enhanced. With modern technology, efficient travel is enhancing career opportunities. It is allowing us to familiarize ourselves with other cultures, different ways of doing things and to learn the positive values of other cultures.

The negative aspects include moral and ethical values, as increased awareness is allowing for a new wave of thinking. Care must be exercised regarding how much of our past culture we are willing to trade for the modern ideas. Positive aspects of any culture must be guarded carefully and passed on to generations to come.

On the whole, we can safely conclude that science and technology are part of our lives and we must always exercise caution and be careful when we are adapting to new ideas and new thinking. It is possible that awareness and incorporation of other cultural practices will make us a better nation, which our founding fathers envisioned and dreamed of.

Effects of scientific and technological breakthroughs on other fields of study, careers, and job markets

Scientific and technological breakthroughs greatly influence other fields of study and the job market. All academic disciplines utilize computer and information technology to simplify research and information sharing. In addition, advances in science and technology influence the types of available jobs and the desired work skills. For example, machines and computers continue to replace unskilled laborers and computer and technological literacy is now a requirement for many jobs and careers. Finally, science and technology continue to change the very nature of careers. Because of science and technology's great influence on all areas of the economy, and the continuing scientific and technological breakthroughs, careers are far less stable than in past eras. Workers can thus expect to change jobs and companies much more often than in the past.

Issues related to science and technology at the local, state, national, and global levels (e.g., environmental policies, genetic research)

Local, state, national, and global governments and organizations must increasingly consider policy issues related to science and technology. For example, local and state governments must analyze the impact of proposed development and growth on the environment. Governments and communities must balance the demands of an expanding human population with the local ecology to ensure sustainable growth.

In addition, advances in science and technology create challenges and ethical dilemmas that national governments and global organizations must attempt to solve. Genetic research and manipulation, antibiotic resistance, stem cell research, and cloning are but a few of the issues facing national governments and global organizations.

In all cases, policymakers must analyze all sides of an issue and attempt to find a solution that protects society while limiting scientific inquiry as little as possible. For example, policymakers must weigh the potential benefits of stem cell research, genetic engineering, and cloning (ie. medical treatments) against the ethical and scientific concerns surrounding these practices. Also, governments must tackle problems like antibiotic resistance, which can result from the indiscriminate use of medications (i.e. antibiotics), in order to prevent medical treatments from becoming obsolete.

Ethics

To understand scientific ethics, we need to have a clear understanding of ethics. Ethics is defined as a system of public, general rules for guiding human conduct (Gert, 1988). The rules are general in that they are supposed to all people at all times and they are public in that they are not secret codes or practices. Scientists are expected to show good conduct in their scientific pursuits. Conduct refers to all aspects of scientific activity including experimentation, testing, education, data evaluation, data analysis, data storing, peer review and government funding.

The following are some of the guiding principles of scientific ethics:

1. Scientific Honesty: not to fraud, fabricate or misinterpret data for personal gain
2. Caution: to avoid errors and sloppiness in all scientific experimentation
3. Credit: give credit where credit is due and not to copy
4. Responsibility: to report only reliable information to the public and not to mislead in the name of science
5. Freedom: freedom to criticize old ideas, question new research and freedom to research

To discuss scientific ethics, we can look at natural phenomena like rain. Rain in the normal sense is extremely useful to us and it is absolutely important that there is a water cycle. When rain gets polluted from car exhaust, it becomes acid rain. Here lies the ethical issue of releasing all these pollutants into the atmosphere. Should the scientists communicate the whole truth about acid rain or withhold some information because it may alarm the public. Whatever may be the case, scientists are expected to be honest and forthright with the public.

Pollution

Pollution includes environmental **contamination by chemical, physical, biological, and radioactive substances**. Major types of pollution include:

Air pollution- The release of a variety of chemicals and particulates causes air pollution. These include carbon monoxide, sulfur dioxide and chlorofluorocarbons (CFC's) as well as carbon particulates. The release of compounds derived from sulfur and nitrogen impurities in fossil fuels contribute to air pollution. Smog is a particular type of air pollution caused by a reaction between sunlight and compounds such as nitrogen oxide and volatile organic compounds which leads to the brown haze over large cities.

Water pollution- Contaminants enter the water system either by ground runoff or by leaching. Historically, industrial waste was dumped directly into bodies of water, but this is more regulated now. However, agricultural runoff continues to pollute water supplies. Buried waste, such as that in landfills, may also leach harmful substances into the soil and groundwater.

Thermal pollution- While industrial facilities typically no longer dispose of contaminants into bodies of water, they may dump water at high temperatures back into the environment. The very hot water both increases temperatures above normal and decreases the concentration of dissolved gases, since gases are less soluble in warm water. Both of these effects are disruptive to the local ecosystem.

Radioactive contamination- Radioactive waste from medical research, and power plant facilities has not always been carefully handled. Accidental leakage and failure to adequately contain waste has led to radioactive pollution in both water and soil.

In addition to certain processes releasing these contaminants into the environment there are secondary effects. For instance, many harmful effects have resulted from the combustion of fossil fuels to produce energy for industrial, commercial, and residential facilities as well as to power many types of automobiles. If pure hydrocarbons are burned in oxygen, the only products of combustion are carbon dioxide and water. However, combustion is typically done in air so nitrogen is also present during the reaction resulting in the formation of nitrous oxides. Impurities in the fuel itself mean that compounds such as sulfur dioxide are also formed during combustion. Finally, incomplete combustion releases carbon monoxide. The following are a few of the known detrimental effects of fossil fuel combustion:

Greenhouse gases- While many "greenhouse gases" such as carbon dioxide and nitrous oxide are naturally occurring, their concentration in the atmosphere has dramatically increased as result of fossil fuel use. Greenhouse gases absorb and trap heat, thus warming the planet and possibly triggering climate change.

Acid rain- Sulfur and nitrous oxides are converted to sulfuric and nitric acid in rain. At sufficient concentrations, they will significantly lower the pH of the rain. This acid rain damages man-made and natural structures. Worse yet, it contaminates our planet's water supplies, damaging not only lakes and rivers and their ecosystems but also groundwater and forests.

Career Opportunities in Science

Science is an interesting, innovative, and thoroughly enjoyable subject. Science careers are challenging and stimulating. The possibilities for scientific careers are endless. Currently, the sky is the limit for opportunities in science for anybody who is interested in that kind of challenge.

Why do people choose careers in science?
This is a very important question. The reasons are manifold and include some of the following:
1. A passion for science
2. A desire to experiment and gain knowledge and/ or contribute to society's betterment
3. An inquiring mind
4. Wanting to work in a team

There are a number of opportunities in science. For the sake of ease and convenience, they are grouped under various categories:
1. Biological sciences
2. Physical sciences
3. Earth science
4. Space science
5. Forensic science
6. Medical science
7. Agricultural science

Let's take each category and examine the opportunities available.

1. Biological Sciences deal with the study of living organisms and their life cycles, medicinal properties etc. People who are interested in studying living things opt for these kinds of careers.
* Botanist - studies plants, for someone who is interested in plants
* Microbiologist: studies microscopic organisms, their uses, harmful effects, and diseases they cause.

2. Physical Science includes careers dealing with various branches of Physical Science (the study of matter, energy etc.)
* Analytical Chemist
* Biochemist
* Chemist
* Physicist

3 Earth Science involves studying the earth, its changes over the years and natural disasters such as earthquakes and hurricanes.
* Geologist
* Meteorologist
* Oceanographer
* Seismologist
* Volcanologist

4. Space Science deals with studying space, the universe and planets. Somebody who is very strong in math and physics and who wants to know about space go for these opportunities.
* Astrophysicist
* Space Scientist

5. Forensic Science involves solving crimes using various techniques.
* Forensic Pathologist

6. Medical Science
* Biomedical science
* Clinical Scientist

7. Agricultural science
* Agriculturist: grows crops using modern methods
* Agricultural Service Industry: the business side of agriculture including marketing
* Agronomists study soil, also known as a Soil Scientist
* Veterinary science: deals with the study and care of animals

There are so many career opportunities available to our youngsters, but it is up to them to choose the right career. The students need to be made aware of the connection between today's learning and their future life. It is especially important to impress upon them how science is everywhere, and its truly useful applications. When this is made clear to them, they will more seriously consider science as a career.

COMPETENCY 3.0   USING KNOWLEDGE OF LIFE SCIENCE

Skill 3.1   Recognize and describe basic concepts of cell biology

The cell is the basic unit of all living things. There are three types of cells. They are prokaryotes, eukaryotes, and archaea. Archaea have some similarities with prokaryotes, but are as distantly related to prokaryotes as prokaryotes are to eukaryotes.

PROKARYOTES

Prokaryotes consist only of bacteria and cyanobacteria (formerly known as blue-green algae). The classification of prokaryotes is in the diagram below.

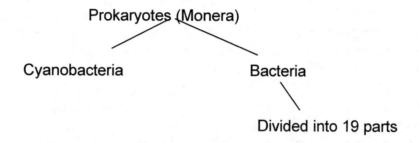

These cells have no defined nucleus or nuclear membrane. The DNA, RNA, and ribosomes float freely within the cell. The cytoplasm has a single chromosome condensed to form a **nucleoid**. Prokaryotes have a thick cell wall made up of amino sugars (glycoproteins). This is for protection, to give the cell shape, and to keep the cell from bursting. It is the **cell wall** of bacteria that is targeted by the antibiotic penicillin. Penicillin works by disrupting the cell wall, thus killing the cell.

The cell wall surrounds the **cell membrane** (plasma membrane). The cell membrane consists of a lipid bilayer that controls the passage of molecules in and out of the cell. Some prokaryotes have a capsule made of polysaccharides that surrounds the cell wall for extra protection from higher organisms.

Many bacterial cells have appendages used for movement called **flagella**. Some cells also have **pili**, which are a protein strand used for attachment of the bacteria. Pili may also be used for sexual conjugation (where the DNA from one bacterial cell is transferred to another bacterial cell).

Prokaryotes are the most numerous and widespread organisms on earth. Bacteria were most likely the first cells and date back in the fossil record to 3.5 billion years ago. Their ability to adapt to the environment allows them to thrive in a wide variety of habitats.

EUKARYOTES

Eukaryotic cells are found in protists, fungi, plants, and animals. Most eukaryotic cells are larger than prokaryotic cells. They contain many organelles, which are membrane bound areas for specific functions. Their cytoplasm contains a cytoskeleton which provides a protein framework for the cell. The cytoplasm also supports the organelles and contains the ions and molecules necessary for cell function. The cytoplasm is contained by the plasma membrane. The plasma membrane allows molecules to pass in and out of the cell. The membrane can bud inward to engulf outside material in a process called endocytosis. Exocytosis is a secretory mechanism, the reverse of endocytosis.

The most significant differentiation between prokaryotes and eukaryotes is that eukaryotes have a **nucleus**. The nucleus is the brain of the cell that contains all of the cell's genetic information. The chromosomes consist of chromatin, which is a complex of DNA and proteins. The chromosomes are tightly coiled to conserve space while providing a large surface area. The nucleus is the site of transcription of the DNA into RNA. The **nucleolus** is where ribosomes are made. There is at least one of these dark-staining bodies inside the nucleus of most eukaryotes. The nuclear envelope consists of two membranes separated by a narrow space. The envelope contains many pores that let RNA out of the nucleus.

Ribosomes are the site for protein synthesis. Ribosomes may be free floating in the cytoplasm or attached to the endoplasmic reticulum. There may be up to a half a million ribosomes in a cell, depending on how much protein is made by the cell.

The **endoplasmic reticulum** (ER) is folded and provides a large surface area. It is the "roadway" of the cell and allows for transport of materials through and out of the cell. There are two types of ER. Smooth endoplasmic reticulum contains no ribosomes on their surface. This is the site of lipid synthesis. Rough endoplasmic reticulum have ribosomes on their surfaces. They aid in the synthesis of proteins that are membrane bound or destined for secretion.

Many of the products made in the ER proceed on to the Golgi apparatus. The **Golgi apparatus** functions to sort, modify, and package molecules that are made in the other parts of the cell (like the ER). These molecules are either sent out of the cell or to other organelles within the cell. The Golgi apparatus is a stacked structure to increase the surface area.

Lysosomes are found mainly in animal cells. These contain digestive enzymes that break down food, substances not needed, viruses, damaged cell components and eventually the cell itself. It is believed that lysomomes are responsible for the aging process.

Mitochondria are large organelles that are the site of cellular respiration, where ATP is made to supply energy to the cell. Muscle cells have many mitochondria because they use a great deal of energy. Mitochondria have their own DNA, RNA, and ribosomes and are capable of reproducing by binary fission if there is a greater demand for additional energy. Mitochondria have two membranes: a smooth outer membrane and a folded inner membrane. The folds inside the mitochondria are called cristae. They provide a large surface area for cellular respiration to occur.

Plastids are found only in photosynthetic organisms. They are similar to the mitochondira due to the double membrane structure. They also have their own DNA, RNA, and ribosomes and can reproduce if the need for the increased capture of sunlight becomes necessary. There are several types of plastids. **Chloroplasts** are the sight of photosynthesis. The stroma is the chloroplast's inner membrane space. The stroma encloses sacs called thylakoids that contain the photosynthetic pigment chlorophyll. The chlorophyll traps sunlight inside the thylakoid to generate ATP which is used in the stroma to produce carbohydrates and other products. The **chromoplasts** make and store yellow and orange pigments. They provide color to leaves, flowers, and fruits. The **amyloplasts** store starch and are used as a food reserve. They are abundant in roots like potatoes.

The Endosymbiotic Theory states that mitochondria and chloroplasts were once free living and possibly evolved from prokaryotic cells. At some point in our evolutionary history, they entered the eukaryotic cell and maintained a symbiotic relationship with the cell, with both the cell and organelle benefiting from the relationship. The fact that they both have their own DNA, RNA, ribosomes, and are capable of reproduction helps to confirm this theory.

Found in plant cells only, the **cell wall** is composed of cellulose and fibers. It is thick enough for support and protection, yet porous enough to allow water and dissolved substances to enter. **Vacuoles** are found mostly in plant cells. They hold stored food and pigments. Their large size allows them to fill with water in order to provide turgor pressure. Lack of turgor pressure causes a plant to wilt.

The **cytoskeleton**, found in both animal and plant cells, is composed of protein filaments attached to the plasma membrane and organelles. They provide a framework for the cell and aid in cell movement. They constantly change shape and move about. Three types of fibers make up the cytoskeleton:

1. **Microtubules** – the largest of the three, they make up cilia and flagella for locomotion. Some examples are sperm cells, cilia that line the fallopian tubes and tracheal cilia. Centrioles are also composed of microtubules. They aid in cell division to form the spindle fibers that pull the chromosomes apart to form two new cells. Centrioles are not found in the cells of higher plants.

2. **Intermediate filaments** – intermediate in size, they are smaller than microtubules but larger than microfilaments. They help the cell to keep its shape.

3. **Microfilaments** – smallest of the three, they are made of actin and small amounts of myosin (like in muscle tissue). They function in cell movement like cytoplasmic streaming, endocytosis, and ameboid movement. This structure pinches the two cells apart after cell division, forming two new cells.

The following is a diagram of a generalized animal cell.

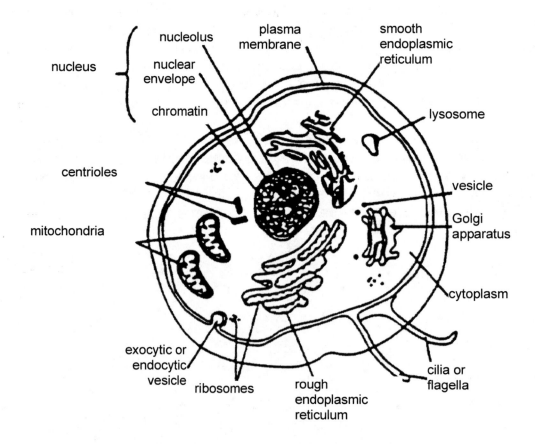

ARCHAEA

There are three kinds of organisms with archaea cells: **methanogens** are obligate anaerobes that produce methane, **halobacteria** can live only in concentrated brine solutions, and **thermoacidophiles** can only live in acidic hot springs.

Animal cells can be described as having a round body inside the cell called the nucleus. It controls the cell's activities. The nucleus contains threadlike structures called chromosomes. The genes are units that control cell activities and are found on the chromosomes. The cytoplasm has many structures in it. Some vacuoles contain the food for the cell. Other vacuoles contain waste materials. Animal cells differ from plant cells because they have centrioles.

Plant cells – have cell walls. A cell wall differs from cell membranes. The cell membrane is very thin and is a part of the cell. The cell wall is thick and is a nonliving part of the cell. Chloroplasts are other structures not found in animals. They are little bundles of chlorophyll used for photosynthesis. The structure of the cell is often related to the cell's function. Root hair cells differ from flower stamens or leaf epidermal cells. They all have different functions.

Single cells – A single cell organism is called a **protist.** When you look under a microscope the animal-like protists are called **protozoans.** They do not have chloroplasts. They are usually classified by the way they move for food. Amoebas engulf other protists by flowing around and over them. The paramecium has a hair like structure which allows it to move back and forth like tiny oars searching for food. The euglena is an example of a protozoan that moves with a tail-like structure called a flagella. Plant-like protists have cell walls and float in water.

Bacteria are the simplest microorganisms. A bacterial cell is surrounded by a cell wall, but there is no nucleus inside the cell. Most bacteria do not contain chlorophyll so they do not make their own food. The classification of bacteria is by shape. Cocci are round, bacilli are rod-shaped, and spirilla are spiral shaped.

Skill 3.2 Analyze the characteristics and life processes of living organisms

Several characteristics have been described to identify living versus non-living substance.
1. Living things are made of cells; they grow, are capable of reproduction and respond to stimuli.
2. Living things must adapt to environmental changes or perish.
3. Living things carry on metabolic processes. They use and make energy.

Multicellular organisms grow via cell growth and reproduction. The purpose of cell division is to provide growth and repair in body (somatic) cells and to replenish or create sex cells for reproduction. There are two forms of cell division. Mitosis is the division of somatic cells and **meiosis** is the division of sex cells (eggs and sperm). The table below summarizes the major differences between the two processes.

MITOSIS	**MEIOSIS**
1. Division of somatic cell	1. Division of sex cells
2. Two cells result from each division	2. Four cells or polar bodies result from each division
3. Chromosome number is identical to parent cells.	3. Chromosome number is half the number of parent cells
4. For cell growth and repair	4. Recombinations provide genetic diversity

Some terms to know:

gamete - sex cell or germ cell; eggs and sperm.
chromatin - loose chromosomes; this state is found when the cell is not dividing.
chromosome - tightly coiled, visible chromatin; this state is found when the cell is dividing.
homologues - chromosomes that contain the same information. They are of the same length and contain the same genes.
diploid - 2n number; diploid chromosomes are a pair of chromosomes (somatic cells).
haploid - 1n number; haploid chromosomes are a half of a pair (sex cells).

MITOSIS

The cell cycle is the life cycle of the cell. It is divided into two stages; **Interphase** and the **mitotic division** where the cell is actively dividing. Interphase is divided into three steps; G1 (growth) period, where the cell is growing and metabolizing, S period (synthesis) where new DNA and enzymes are being made and the G2 phase (growth) where new proteins and organelles are being made to prepare for cell division. The mitotic stage consists of the stages of mitosis and the division of the cytoplasm. The stages of mitosis and their events are as follows. Be sure to know the correct order of steps. (IPMAT)

1. Interphase - chromatin is loose, chromosomes are replicated, cell metabolism is occurring. Interphase is technically <u>not</u> a stage of mitosis

2. Prophase - once the cell enters prophase, it proceeds through the following steps continuously, with no stopping. The chromatin condenses to become visible chromosomes. The nucleolus disappears and the nuclear membrane breaks apart. Mitotic spindles form that will eventually pull the chromosomes apart. They are composed of microtubules. The cytoskeleton breaks down and the spindles are pushed to the poles or opposite ends of the cell by the action of centrioles.

3. Metaphase - kinetechore fibers attach to the chromosomes which causes the chromosomes to line up in the center of the cell (think **m**iddle for **m**etaphase)

4. Anaphase - centromeres split in half and homologous chromosomes separate. The chromosomes are pulled to the poles of the cell, with identical sets at either end.

5. Telophase - two nuclei form with a full set of DNA that is identical to the parent cell. The nucleoli become visible and the nuclear membrane reassembles. A cell plate is visible in plant cells, whereas a cleavage furrow is formed in animal cells. The cell is pinched into two cells. Cytokinesis, or division, of the cytoplasm and organelles occurs.

Meiosis contains the same five stages as mitosis, but is repeated in order to reduce the chromosome number by one half. This way, when the sperm and egg join during fertilization, the diploid number is reached. The steps of meiosis are as follows:

Major function of Meiosis I – Diploid germ cells become haploid .

Prophase I - replicated chromosomes condense and pair with homologues. This forms a tetrad. Crossing over (the exchange of genetic material between homologues to further increase diversity) occurs during Prophase I.
Metaphase I - homologous sets attach to spindle fibers after lining up in the middle of the cell.
Anaphase I - sister chromatids remain joined and move to the poles of the cell.
Telophase I - two new cells are formed, chromosome number is now haploid

Major function of Meiosis II - to reduce the chromosome number in half.

Prophase II - chromosomes condense.
Metaphase II - spindle fibers form again, sister chromatids line up in center of cell, centromeres divide and sister chromatids separate.
Anaphase II - separated chromosomes move to opposite ends of cell.
Telophase II - four haploid cells form for each original sperm germ cell. One viable egg cell gets all the genetic information and three polar bodies form with no DNA. The nuclear membrane reforms and cytokinesis occurs.

Plant Tissues

Specialization of tissue enabled plants to get larger. Be familiar with the following tissues and their functions:

Xylem - transports water.

Phloem - transports food (glucose).

Cortex - storage of food and water.

Epidermis – protection.

Endodermis - controls movement between the cortex and the cell interior.

Pericycle - meristematic tissue that can divide when necessary.

Pith - storage in stems.

Sclerenchyma and collenchyma - support in stems.

Stomata - openings on the underside of leaves. They let carbon dioxide in and water out (transpiration).

Guard cells - control the size of the stomata. If the plant has to conserve water, the stomates will close.

Palisade mesophyll - contain chloroplasts in leaves. Site of photosynthesis.

Spongy mesophyll - open spaces in the leaf that allows for gas circulation.

Seed coat - protective covering on a seed.

Cotyledon - small seed leaf that emerges when the seed germinates.

Endosperm - food supply in the seed.

Apical meristem - this is an area of cell division allowing for growth.

Flowers are the reproductive organs of the plant. Know the following functions and locations:

Pedicel - supports the weight of the flower.

Receptacle - holds the floral organs at the base of the flower.

Sepals - green leaf like parts that cover the flower prior to blooming.

Petals - contain coloration by pigments to attract insects to assist in pollination.

Anther - male part that produces pollen.

Filament - supports the anther; the filament and anther make up the stamen.

Stigma - female part that holds pollen grains that came from the male part.

Style - tube that leads to the ovary (female).

Ovary - contains the ovules; the stigma, style and ovary make up the carpel.

Plant physiological processes

Photosynthesis is the process by which plants make carbohydrates from the energy of the sun, carbon dioxide and water. Oxygen is a waste product. Photosynthesis occurs in the chloroplast where the pigment chlorophyll traps sun energy. It is divided into two major steps:

Light Reactions - Sunlight is trapped, water is split, and oxygen is given off. ATP is made and hydrogens reduce NADP to $NADPH_2$. The light reactions occur in light. The products of the light reactions enter into the dark reactions (Calvin cycle).

Dark Reactions - Carbon dioxide enters during the dark reactions which can occur with or without the presence of light. The energy transferred from $NADPH_2$ and ATP allow for the fixation of carbon into glucose.

Respiration - during times of decreased light, plants break down the products of photosynthesis through cellular respiration. Glucose, with the help of oxygen breaks down and produces carbon dioxide and water as wastes. Approximately fifty percent of the products of photosynthesis are used by the plant for energy.

Transpiration - water travels up the xylem of the plant through the process of transpiration. Water sticks to itself (cohesion) and to the walls of the xylem (adhesion). As it evaporates through the stomata of the leaves, the water is pulled up the column from the roots. Environmental factors such as heat and wind increase the rate of transpiration. High humidity will decrease the rate of transpiration.

Reproduction - Angiosperms are the largest group in the plant kingdom. They are the flowering plants and produce true seeds for reproduction. They arose about seventy million years ago when the dinosaurs were disappearing. The land was drying up and their ability to produce seeds that could remain dormant until conditions became acceptable and allowed for their success. They also had more advanced vascular tissue and larger leaves for increased photosynthesis. Angiosperms reproduce through a method of **double fertilization**. An ovum is fertilized by two sperm. One sperm produces they new plant, the other forms the food supply for the developing plant.

Seed dispersal - success of plant reproduction involves the seed moving away from the parent plant to decrease competition for space, water and minerals. Seeds may be carried by wind (maples), water (palms), carried by animals (burrs) or ingested by animals and released in their feces in another area.

Organization

Life is highly organized. The organization of living systems builds on levels from small to increasingly more large and complex. All aspects, whether it is a cell or an ecosystem, have the same requirements to sustain life. Life is organized from simple to complex in the following way:

Atoms→molecules→organelles→cells→tissues→organs→organ systems→organism

Functions of major organs in animals

Skeletal System - The skeletal system functions in support. Vertebrates have an endoskeleton, with muscles attached to bones. Skeletal proportions are controlled by area to volume relationships. Body size and shape is limited due to the forces of gravity. Surface area is increased to improve efficiency in all organ systems.

Muscular System - function is for movement. There are three types of muscle tissue. Skeletal muscle is voluntary. These muscles are attached to bones. Smooth muscle is involuntary. It is found in organs and enable functions such as digestion and respiration. Cardiac muscle is a specialized type of smooth muscle.

Nervous System - The neuron is the basic unit of the nervous system. It consists of an axon, which carries impulses away from the cell body, the dendrite, which carries impulses toward the cell body and the cell body, which contains the nucleus. Synapses are spaces between neurons. Chemicals called neurotransmitters are found close to the synapse. The myelin sheath is composed of Schwann cells and covers the neurons to provide insulation.

Digestive System - The function of the digestive system is to break down food and absorb it into the blood stream where it can be delivered to all cells of the body for use in cellular respiration. As animals evolved, digestive systems changed from simple absorption to a system with a separate mouth and anus, capable of allowing the animal to become independent of a host.

Respiratory System - This system functions in the gas exchange of needed oxygen and carbon dioxide waste. It delivers oxygen to the bloodstream and picks up carbon dioxide for release out of the body. Simple animals diffuse gases from and to their environment. Gills allowed aquatic animals to exchange gases in a fluid medium by removing dissolved oxygen from the water. Lungs maintained a fluid environment for gas exchange in terrestrial animals.

Circulatory System - The function of the circulatory system is to carry oxygenated blood and nutrients to all cells of the body and return carbon dioxide waste to be expelled from the lungs. Animals evolved from an open system to a closed system with vessels leading to and from the heart.

Major physiological processes in animals

Homeostasis- The molecular composition of the immediate environment outside of the organism is not the same as it is inside and the temperature outside may not be optimal for metabolic activity within the organism. **Homeostasis** is the control of these differences between internal and external environments. There are three homeostatic systems to regulate these differences.

Osmoregulation deals with maintenance of the appropriate level of water and salts in body fluids for optimum cellular functions. **Excretion** is the elimination of metabolic waste products from the body including excess water. **Thermoregulation** maintains the internal, or core, body temperature of the organism within a tolerable range for metabolic and cellular processes.

Animal respiration takes in oxygen and gives off waste gases. For instance a fish uses its gills to extract oxygen from the water. Bubbles are evidence that waste gases are expelled. Respiration without oxygen is called anaerobic respiration. Anaerobic respiration in animal cells is also called lactic acid fermentation. The end product is lactic acid.

Animal reproduction can be asexual or sexual. Geese lay eggs. Animals such as bear cubs, deer, and rabbits are born alive. Some animals reproduce frequently, others do not. Some animals only produce one baby while others produce many.

Animal digestion – some animals only eat meat while others only eat plants. Many animals do both. Nature has created animals with structural adaptations so they may obtain food through sharp teeth or long facial structures. Digestion's purpose is to break down carbohydrates, fats and proteins. Many organs are needed to digest food starting with the mouth. Certain animals such as birds have beaks to puncture wood or allow for large fish to be consumed. The tooth structure of a beaver is designed to cut down trees. Tigers are known for their sharp teeth used to rip hides from their prey. Enzymes are catalysts that help speed up chemical reactions by lowering effective activation energy. Enzyme rate is affected by temperature, pH, and the amount of substrate. Saliva contains the enzyme amylase that changes starches into sugars.

Animal circulation – The blood temperature of all mammals stays constant regardless of the outside temperature (within reason). This is called warm-blooded, while cold-blooded animals circulation will vary with the temperature.

Skill 3.3 Explain basic principles and theories related to the inheritance of characteristics

Chromosomes are the physical structures found in every cell which carry the genetic information of an organism and function in the transmission of hereditary information. Each chromosome contains a sequence of genes each with a specific locus. A locus is the position a given gene occupies on a chromosome. Each gene consists of a sequence of DNA that dictates a particular characteristic of an organism. Separating the genes on a chromosome are regions of DNA that do not code for proteins or other cellular products, but may function in the regulation of coding regions.

Gregor Mendel is recognized as the father of genetics. His work in the late 1800's is the basis of our knowledge of genetics. Although unaware of the presence of DNA or genes, Mendel realized there were factors (now known as genes) that were transferred from parents to their offspring. Mendel worked with pea plants and fertilized the plants himself, keeping track of subsequent generations which led to the Mendelian laws of genetics. Mendel found that two "factors" governed each trait, one from each parent. Traits or characteristics came in several forms, known as alleles. For example, the trait of flower color had white alleles and purple alleles. Mendel formed three laws:

Law of dominance - in a pair of alleles, one trait may cover up the allele of the other trait. Example: brown eyes are dominant to blue eyes.

Law of segregation - only one of the two possible alleles from each parent is passed on to the offspring from each parent. (During meiosis, the haploid number insures that half the sex cells get one allele, half get the other).

Law of independent assortment - alleles sort independently of each other. Many combinations are possible depending on which sperm ends up with which egg (compare this to the many combinations of hands possible when dealing a deck of cards).

monohybrid cross - a cross using only one trait.

dihybrid cross - a cross using two traits. More combinations are possible.

Punnet squares - these are used to show the possible ways that genes combine or probability of the occurrence of a certain genotype or phenotype. One parent's genes are put at the top of the box and the other parent at the side of the box. Genes combine on the square just like numbers that are added in addition tables that we learned in elementary school.

Example: Monohybrid Cross - four possible gene combinations

Example: Dihybrid Cross - sixteen possible gene combinations

SOME DEFINITIONS TO KNOW -

Dominant - the stronger of the two traits. If a dominant gene is present, it will be expressed. Shown by a capital letter.

Recessive - the weaker of the two traits. In order for the recessive gene to be expressed, there must be two recessive genes present. Shown by a lower case letter.

Homozygous - (purebred) having two of the same genes present; an organism may be homozygous dominant with two dominant genes or homozygous recessive with two recessive genes.

Heterozygous - (hybrid) having one dominant gene and one recessive gene. The dominant gene will be expressed due to the Law of Dominance.

Genotype - the genes the organism has. Genes are represented with letters. AA, Bb, and tt are examples of genotypes.

Phenotype - how the trait is expressed in an organism. Blue eyes, brown hair, and red flowers are examples of phenotypes.

Incomplete dominance - neither gene masks the other; a new phenotype is formed. For example, red flowers and white flowers may have equal strength. A heterozygote (Rr) would have pink flowers. If a problem occurs with a third phenotype, incomplete dominance is occurring.

Codominance - genes may form new phenotypes. The ABO blood grouping is an example of co-dominance. A and B are of equal strength and O is recessive. Therefore, type A blood may have the genotypes of AA or AO, type B blood may have the genotypes of BB or BO, type AB blood has the genotype A and B, and type O blood has two recessive O genes.

Linkage - genes that are found on the same chromosome usually appear together unless crossing over has occurred in meiosis. (Example - blue eyes and blonde hair)

Lethal alleles - these are usually recessive due to the early death of the offspring. If a 2:1 ratio of alleles is found in offspring, a lethal gene combination is usually the reason. Some examples of lethal alleles include sickle cell anemia, tay-sachs and cystic fibrosis. Usually the coding for an important protein is affected.

Inborn errors of metabolism - these occur when the protein affected is an enzyme. Examples include PKU (phenylketonuria) and albanism.

Polygenic characters - many alleles code for a phenotype. There may be as many as twenty genes that code for skin color. This is why there is such a variety of skin tones. Another example is height. A couple of medium height may have very tall offspring.

Sex linked traits - the Y chromosome found only in males (XY) carries very little genetic information, whereas the X chromosome found in females (XX) carries very important information. Since men have no second X chromosome to cover up a recessive gene, the recessive trait is expressed more often in men. Women need the recessive gene on both X chromosomes to show the trait. Examples of sex linked traits include hemophilia and color-blindness.

Sex influenced traits - traits are influenced by the sex hormones. Male pattern baldness is an example of a sex influenced trait. Testosterone influences the expression of the gene. Mostly men lose their hair due to this.

Mutations

Since it's not a perfect world, mistakes happen. Inheritable changes in DNA are called **mutations**. Mutations may be errors in replication or a spontaneous rearrangement of one or more segments by factors like radioactivity, drugs, or chemicals. The amount of the change is not as critical as where the change is. Mutations may occur on somatic or sex cells. Usually the ones on sex cells are more dangerous since they contain the basis of all information for the developing offspring. Mutations are not always bad. They are the basis of evolution, and if they make a more favorable variation that enhances the organism's survival, then they are beneficial. But, mutations may also lead to abnormalities, birth defects, and even death. There are several types of mutations; let's suppose a normal DNA sequence was as follows:

Normal: A B C D E F

Duplication - one base is repeated.   A B C C D E F

Inversion - a segment of the sequence is flipped around. A E D C B F

Deletion - a base is left out. A B C E F

Insertion or Translocation - a segment from another place on the DNA is stuck in the wrong place.   A B C R S D E F

Breakage - a piece is lost. A B C (DEF is lost)

Nondisjunction - during meiosis, chromosomes fail to separate properly. One sex cell may get both chromosomes and another may get none. Depending on the chromosomes involved this may or may not be serious. Offspring end up with either an extra chromosome or are missing one. An example of nondisjunction is Down Syndrome, where three #21 chromosomes are present.

Environmental Influence

Environmental factors can influence the structure and expression of genes. For instance, viruses can insert their DNA into the host's genome changing the composition of the host DNA. In addition, mutagenic agents found in the environment cause mutations in DNA and carcinogenic agents promote cancer, often by causing DNA mutations.

Many viruses can insert their DNA into the host genome causing mutations. Many times viral insertion of DNA does not harm the host DNA because of the location of the insertion. Some insertions, however, can have grave consequences for the host. Oncogenes are genes that increase the malignancy of tumor cells. Some viruses carry oncogenes that, when inserted into the host genome, become active and promote cancerous growth. In addition, insertion of other viral DNA into the host genome can stimulate expression of host proto-oncogenes, genes that normally promote cell division. For example, insertion of a strong viral promoter in front of a host proto-oncogene may stimulate expression of the gene and lead to uncontrolled cell growth (i.e. cancer).

In addition to viruses, physical and chemical agents found in the environment can damage gene structure. Mutagenic agents cause mutations in DNA. Examples of mutagenic agents are x-rays, UV light, and ethidium bromide. Carcinogenic agents are any substances that promote cancer. Carcinogens are often, but not always, mutagens. Examples of agents carcinogenic to humans are asbestos, UV light, x-rays, and benzene.

Skill 3.4   Explain basic principles and theories related to the way species change through time

The dominant scientific theory about the origin of the Universe, and consequently the Earth, is the **Big Bang Theory**. According to this theory, a point source exploded about 10 to 20 billion years ago throwing matter in all directions. Although this theory has never been proven, and probably never will be, it is supported by the fact that distant galaxies in every direction are moving away from us at great speeds.

Earth, itself, is believed to have been created 4.5 billion years ago as a solidified cloud of gases and dust left over from the creation of the sun. As millions of years passed, radioactive decay released energy that melted some of Earth's components. Over time, the heavier components sank to the center of the Earth and accumulated into the core. As the Earth cooled, a crust formed with natural depressions. Water rising from the interior of the Earth filled these depressions and formed the oceans. Slowly, the Earth acquired the appearance it has today.

The **Heterotroph Hypothesis** supposes that life on Earth evolved from **heterotrophs**, the first cells. According to this hypothesis, life began on Earth about 3.5 billion years ago. Scientists have shown that the basic molecules of life formed from lightning, ultraviolet light, and radioactivity. Over time, these molecules became more complex and developed metabolic processes, thereby becoming heterotrophs. Heterotrophs could not produce their own food and fed off organic materials. However, they released carbon dioxide which allowed for the evolution of **autotrophs**, which could produce their own food through photosynthesis. The autotrophs and heterotrophs became the dominant life forms and evolved into the diverse forms of life we see today.

Proponents of **creationism** believe that the species we currently have were created as recounted in the book of Genesis in the Bible. This retelling asserts that God created all life about 6,000 years ago in one mass creation event. However, scientific evidence casts doubt on creationism.

Evolution

The most significant evidence to support the history of evolution are fossils, which have been used to construct a fossil record. Fossils give clues as to the structure of organisms and the times at which they existed. However, there are limitations to the study of fossils, which leave huge gaps in the fossil record.

Scientists also try to relate two organisms by comparing their internal and external structures. This is called **comparative anatomy**. Comparative anatomy categorizes anatomical structures as **homologous** (features in different species that point to a common ancestor), **analogous** (structures that have superficial similarities because of similar functions, but do not point to a common ancestor), and **vestigial** (structures that have no modern function, indicating that different species diverged and evolved). Through the study of **comparative embryology**, homologous structures that do not appear in mature organisms may be found between different species in their embryological development.

There have been two basic **theories of evolution: Lamarck's and Darwin's**. Lamarck's theory proposed that an organism can change its structure through use or disuse and that acquired traits can be inherited has been disproved.

Darwin's theory of **natural selection** is the basis of all evolutionary theory. His theory has four basic points:

1. Each species produces more offspring than can survive.
2. The individual organisms that make up a larger population are born with certain variations.
3. The overabundance of offspring creates competition for survival among individual organisms (**survival of the fittest**).
4. Variations are passed down from parent to offspring.

Points 2 and 4 form the genetic basis for evolution.

New species develop from two types of evolution: divergent and convergent. **Divergent evolution**, also known as **speciation**, is the divergence of a new species from a previous form of that species. There are two main ways in which speciation may occur: **allopatric speciation** (resulting from geographical isolation so that species cannot interbreed) and **adaptive radiation** (creation of several new species from a single parent species). **Convergent evolution** is a process whereby different species develop similar traits from inhabiting similar environments, facing similar selection pressures, and/or use parts of their bodies for similar functions. This type of evolution is only superficial. It can never result in two species being able to interbreed.

Causes of evolution - Certain factors increase the chances of variability in a population, thus leading to evolution. Items that increase variability include mutations, sexual reproduction, immigration, large population, and variation in geographic local. Items that decrease variation would be natural selection, emigration, small population, and random mating.

Sexual selection - Obviously the genes that happen to come together determine the makeup of the gene pool. Animals that use mating behaviors may be successful or unsuccessful. An animal that lacks attractive plumage or has a weak mating call will not attract the female, thereby eventually limiting that gene in the gene pool. Mechanical isolation, where sex organs do not fit the female, has an obvious disadvantage.

Adaptation

Anatomical structures and physiological processes that evolve over geological time to increase the overall reproductive success of an organism in its environment are known as biological adaptations. Such evolutionary changes occur through natural selection, the process by which individual organisms with favorable traits survive to reproduce more frequently than those with unfavorable traits. The heritable component of such favorable traits is passed down to offspring during reproduction, increasing the frequency of the favorable trait in a population over many generations.

Adaptations increase long-term reproductive success by making an organism better suited for survival under particular environmental conditions and pressures. These biological changes can increase an organism's ability to obtain air, water, food and nutrients, to cope with environmental variables and to defend themselves. The term adaptation may apply to changes in biological processes that, for example, enable on organism to produce venom or to regulate body temperature, and also to structural adaptations, such as an organisms' skin color and shape. Adaptations can occur in behavioral traits and survival mechanisms as well.

One well known structural change that demonstrates the concept of adaptation is the development of the primate and human opposable thumb, the first digit of the hand that can be moved around to touch other digits and to grasp objects. The history of the opposable thumb is one of complexly linked structural and behavioral adaptations in response to environmental stressors.

Early apes first appearing in the Tertiary Period were mostly tree dwelling organisms that foraged for food and avoided predators high above the ground. The apes' need to quickly and effectively navigate among branches led to the eventual development of the opposable thumb through the process of natural selection, as apes with more separated thumbs demonstrated higher survival and reproductive rates. This structural adaptation made the ape better suited for its environment, increasing dexterity while climbing trees, moving through the canopy, gathering food and gripping tools such as sticks and branches.

Following the development of the opposable thumb in primates, populations of early human ancestors began to appear in a savannah environment with fewer trees and more open spaces. The need to cross such expanses and to utilize tools led to the development of bipedalism in certain primates and hominids. Bipedalism was both a structural adaptation in the physical changes that occurred in the skull, spine and other parts of the body to accommodate upright walking, as well as a behavioral adaptation that led primates and hominids to walk on only two feet. Freeing of the hands for tool use led, in turn, to other adaptations, and evolutionists attribute the gradual increase in brain size and expansion of motor skills in hominids largely to the appearance of the opposable thumb. Thus, the developments of the most important adaptations of primates and humans demonstrate closely connected evolutionary histories.

Skill 3.5　Analyze characteristics of populations, communities, ecosystems, and biomes

Ecology is the study of organisms, where they live and their interactions with the environment. A population is a group of the same species in a specific area. A community is a group of populations residing in the same area. Communities that are ecologically similar in regards to temperature, rainfall and the species that live there are called biomes.

Specific biomes include:

Marine - covers seventy-five percent of the earth. This biome is organized by the depth of the water. The intertidal zone is from the tide line to the edge of the water. The littoral zone is from the waters edge to the open sea. It includes coral reef habitats and is the most densely populated area of the marine biome. The open sea zone is divided into the epipelagic zone and the pelagic zone. The epipelagic zone receives more sunlight and has a larger number of species. The ocean floor is called the benthic zone and is populated with bottom feeders.

Tropical Rain Forest - temperature is constant (25 degrees C), rainfall exceeds 200 cm. per year. Located around the area of the equator, the rain forest has abundant, diverse species of plants and animals.

Savanna - temperatures range from 0 - 25 degrees C depending on the location. Rainfall is from 90 to 150 cm per year. Plants include shrubs and grasses. The savanna is a transitional biome between the rain forest and the desert.

Desert - temperatures range from 10 - 38 degrees C. Rainfall is under 25 cm per year. Plant species include xerophytes and succulents. Lizards, snakes and small mammals are common animals.

Temperate Deciduous Forest - temperature ranges from -24 to 38 degrees C. Rainfall is between 65 to 150 cm per year. Deciduous trees are common, as well as deer, bear and squirrels.

Taiga - temperatures range from -24 to 22 degrees C. Rainfall is between 35 to 40 cm per year. Taiga is located very north and very south of the equator, getting close to the poles. Plant life includes conifers and plants that can withstand harsh winters. Animals include weasels, mink, and moose.

Tundra - temperatures range from -28 to 15 degrees C. Rainfall is limited, ranging from 10 to 15 cm per year. The tundra is located even further north and south of the taiga. Common plants include lichens and mosses. Animals include polar bears and musk ox.

Polar or Permafrost - temperature ranges from -40 to 0 degrees C. It rarely gets above freezing. Rainfall is below 10 cm per year. Most water is bound up as ice. Life is limited.

Succession - an orderly process of replacing a community that has been damaged or has begun where no life previously existed. Primary succession occurs after a community has been totally wiped out by a natural disaster or where life never existed before, as in a flooded area. Secondary succession takes place in communities that were once flourishing but disturbed by some source, either man or nature, but not totally stripped. A climax community is a community that is established and flourishing.

Definitions of feeding relationships:

Parasitism - two species that occupy a similar place; the parasite benefits from the relationship, the host is harmed.

Commensalism - two species that occupy a similar place; neither species is harmed or benefits from the relationship.

Mutualism (symbiosis)- two species that occupy a similar place; both species benefit from the relationship.

Competition - two species that occupy the same habitat or eat the same food are said to be in competition with each other.

Predation - animals that eat other animals are called predators. They animals they feed on are called the prey. Population growth depends upon competition for food, water, shelter and space. The amount of predators determines the amount of prey, which in turn affects the number of predators.

Carrying Capacity - this is the total amount of life a habitat can support. Once the habitat runs out of food, water, shelter or space, the carrying capacity decreases, and then stabilizes.

Endangered species - construction to house our overpopulated world has caused a destruction of habitat for other animals leading to extinction.

Overpopulation - the human race is still growing at an exponential rate. Carrying capacity has not been met due to our ability to use technology to produce more food and housing. Space and water can not be manufactured and eventually our overuse affects every living thing on this planet.

Biogeochemical cycles

Essential elements are recycled through an ecosystem. At times, the element needs to be "fixed" in a useable form. Cycles are dependent on plants, algae and bacteria to fix nutrients for use by animals.

Water cycle – Two percent of all the available water is fixed and unavailable in ice or the bodies of organisms. Available water includes surface water (lakes, ocean, and rivers) and ground water (aquifers, wells). Ninety-six percent of all available water is from ground water. Water is recycled through the processes of evaporation and precipitation. The water present now is the water that has been here since our atmosphere formed.

Carbon cycle - Ten percent of all available carbon in the air (from carbon dioxide gas) is fixed by photosynthesis. Plants fix carbon in the form of glucose, animals eat the plants and are able to obtain their source of carbon. When animals release carbon dioxide through respiration, the plants again have a source of carbon to fix again.

Nitrogen cycle - Eighty percent of the atmosphere is in the form of nitrogen gas. Nitrogen must be fixed and taken out of the gaseous form to be incorporated into an organism. Only a few genera of bacteria have the correct enzymes to break the triple bond between nitrogen atoms. These bacteria live within the roots of legumes (peas, beans, alfalfa) and add bacteria to the soil so it may be taken up by the plant. Nitrogen is necessary to make amino acids and the nitrogenous bases of DNA.

Phosphorus cycle - Phosphorus exists as a mineral and is not found in the atmosphere. Fungi and plant roots have a structure called mycorrhizae that are able to fix insoluble phosphates into useable phosphorus. Urine and decayed matter returns phosphorus to the earth where it can be fixed in the plant. Phosphorus is needed for the backbone of DNA and for ATP manufacture.

Energy Transfer

Energy transfer is also a key concept in the creation of food webs and food pyramids. Food webs and pyramids show the feeding relationships between organisms in an ecosystem. The primary producers of an ecosystem produce organic compounds from an energy source and inorganic materials. Primary consumers obtain energy by feeding on producers. Finally, secondary consumers obtain energy by feeding on primary consumers.

Basic requirements for life

All organisms are adapted to life in their unique habitat. The habitat includes all the components of their physical environment and is a necessity for the species' survival. Below are several key components of a complete habitat that all organisms require.

Food and water
Because all biochemical reactions take place in aqueous environments, all organisms must have access to clean water, even if only infrequently. Organisms also require two types of food: a source of energy (fixed carbon) and a source of nutrients. Autotrophs can fix carbon for themselves, but must have access to certain inorganic precursors. These organisms must also be able to obtain other nutrients, such as nitrogen, from their environment. Heterotrophs, on the other hand, must consume other organisms for both energy and nutrients. The species these organisms use as a food source must be present in their habitat.

Sunlight and air

This need is closely related to that for food and water because almost all species derive some needed nutrients from the sun and atmosphere. Plants require carbon dioxide to photosynthesize and oxygen is required for cellular respiration. Sunlight is also necessary for photosynthesis and is used by many animals to synthesize essential nutrients (i.e. vitamin D).

Shelter and space

The need for shelter and space vary greatly between species. Many plants do not need shelter, per se, but must have adequate soil to spread their roots and acquire nutrients. Certain invasive species can threaten native plants by out-competing them for space. Other types of plants and many animals also require protection from environmental hazards. These locations may facilitate reproduction (for instance, nesting sites) or provide seasonal shelter (for examples, dens and caves used by hibernating species).

Biotic and abiotic factors influence population density

Biotic factors - living things in an ecosystem; plants, animals, bacteria, fungi, etc. If one population in a community increases, it affects the ability of another population to succeed by limiting the available amount of food, water, shelter and space.

Abiotic factors - non-living aspects of an ecosystem; soil quality, rainfall, temperature. Changes in climate and soil can cause effects at the beginning of the food chain, thus limiting or accelerating the growth of population.

COMPETENCY 4.0   USING KNOWLEDGE OF PHYSICAL SCIENCE

Skill 4.1   Analyze and describe the structure and nature of matter

Atomic Theory

Atomic theory basically states that atoms are the basic, smallest building units of matter. Atoms themselves are made from **protons, neutrons, and electrons**. The nucleus of the atom is very small in relationship to the atom and much of the atom is actually empty space. The nucleus is the positively charged component of the atom and the neutron has a zero charge. Electrons circle the proton and carry a negative charge. If you break an atom into its smaller parts, you lose the property of the element.

Atoms differ depending upon the elemental form they make. The simplest atom is hydrogen, which has one proton and one electron that are attracted to each other due to an electrical charge. The spinning force of the electron keeps the electron from crashing into the proton and keeps the electron always moving.

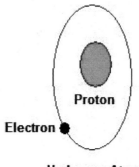

Hydrogen Atom

This is the hydrogen atom, abbreviated H. It has a single neutron and single rotating electron.

Periodic Table

The periodic table tells us a lot about the various elements and their atomic structures. The Periodic table was invented in the late 1800s by Dmitri Mendeleev and clusters all of the known elements by their similar characteristics. He made the Law of Chemical Periodicity which states that the properties of the various elements are functions of the atomic number of the element. Elements are grouped according to different groups and "periods" and are listed in order of their atomic number. The atomic number is equal to the number of protons in each atom. If the element is in its neutral state, the number of electrons is the same as the number of protons.

In a typical periodic table, the atomic number is located below the symbol of the element. The atomic mass number is located below the symbol. The atomic mass number is listed in units called Atomic Mass Units, where 1 AMU equals 1/12 times the mass of carbon in grams. This takes into account both the neutrons and protons in the element. Elements that share the same atomic number but have different atomic mass units are called **isotopes** of one another. The figure below represents the basic unit of the periodic table.

The periodic table is divided into "groups" and "periods". Groups represent the vertical columns that include elements that are similar with respect to their chemical and physical properties. The columns start with metals and progress to nonmetals. The groups are shown as below.

- **Group 1A:** Known as Alkali Metals; Very reactive; Never found free in nature; React readily with water; example would be sodium.

- **Group 2A:** Known as Alkaline earth elements; All are metals; Occur only in compounds; React with oxygen in the general formula EO (where O is oxygen and E is Group 2A element); example is magnesium.

- **Group 3A:** Metalloids; Includes aluminum (the most abundant metal in the earth); Forms oxygen compounds with a X_2O_3 formula.

- **Group 4A:** Includes metals and nonmetals; Go from nonmetals at the top of the column to metals at the bottom; All elements form compounds with a XO_2 formula; Example is carbon.

- **Group 5A:** All elements form an oxygen or sulfur compound with E_2O_3 or E_2S_3 formulas; Example is nitrogen.

- **Group 6A:** Includes oxygen.

- **Group 7A:** Elements combine violently with alkali metals to form salts; all are highly reactive; Includes fluorine and chlorine.

- **Group 8A:** Not abundant on the earth. Called the noble gases because they aren't very reactive. These are minimally-reactive gases like neon and argon.

There are more than one model of the structure of atoms. Niels Bohr created a mode in which the nuclei orbit the nucleus as in a solar system. Each orbit involves a different energy level. This model was later found to be wrong.

The newer model is called the quantum model that states that the electron cannot be precisely found but can be predicted as a sort of probability that any given electron will be at some location in the atom. Quantum numbers are a series of numbers that describe the location of an electron in 3D space. The three numbers are known as "n", which is the principle quantum number that describes the quantum level or shell that the electron resides. The second number is called "l" and is known as the azimuthal quantum number. This tells us the sublevel or subshell in a given atomic orbital. It is always one less than the principal number. The third quantum number is "m" or the magnetic quantum number. It has a value of between -1 and +1 and relates to the way light is emitted in a magnetic field.

Bonding and reactions

Chemical reactions are the interactions of substances resulting in chemical change and change in energy. Chemical reactions involve changes in electron motion and the breaking and forming of chemical bonds. Reactants are the original substances that interact to form distinct products. Endothermic chemical reactions consume energy while exothermic chemical reactions release energy with product formation. Chemical reactions occur continually in nature and are also induced by man for many purposes.

Nuclear reactions, or **atomic reactions**, are reactions that change the composition, energy, or structure of atomic nuclei. Nuclear reactions change the number of protons and neutrons in the nucleus. The two main types of nuclear reactions are fission (splitting of nuclei) and fusion (joining of nuclei). Fusion reactions are exothermic, releasing heat energy. Fission reactions are endothermic, absorbing heat energy. Fission of large nuclei (e.g. uranium) releases energy because the products of fission undergo further fusion reactions. Fission and fusion reactions can occur naturally, but are most recognized as man-made events. Particle acceleration and bombardment with neutrons are two methods of inducing nuclear reactions.

Formulas

A formula is a shorthand of showing what is in a compound by using symbols and subscripts. The letter symbols let us know the elements that are involved and the number subscripts tell us how many atoms of each element are involved. No subscript is used if there is only one atom involved.

For example – CH_4 – This compound is methane gas and it has one carbon atom and 4 hydrogen atoms.

Stoichiometry is the calculation of quantitative relationships between reactants and products in chemical reactions. Scientists use stoichiometry to balance chemical equations, make conversions between units of measurement (e.g. grams to moles), and determine the correct amount of reactants to use in chemical reactions.

Example:

The reaction of iron (Fe) and hydrochloric acid (HCl) produces H_2 and $FeCl_2$. Determine the amount of HCl required to react with 200g of Fe.

$Fe + HCl = H_2 + FeCl_2$

$Fe + 2HCl = H_2 + FeCl_2$ Balance equation (equal number of atoms on each side)

$$\frac{200g\ \text{Fe}}{1} \cdot \frac{1\ mol\ \text{Fe}}{55.8g\ \text{Fe}} \cdot \frac{2\ mol\ \text{HCl}}{1\ mol\ \text{Fe}} \cdot \frac{36.5g\ \text{HCl}}{1\ mol\ \text{HCl}}$$ Perform stoichiometric calculations

= 262 g of HCl required to react completely with 200 g Fe   Solve

Instruments

Scientists utilize various instruments and technologies to study matter and energy. Commonly used instruments include spectrometers, basic measuring devices, thermometers, and calorimeters.

Spectroscopy is the study of absorption and emission of energy of different frequencies by molecules and atoms. The spectrometer is the instrument used in spectroscopy. Because different molecules and atoms have different spectroscopic properties, spectroscopy helps scientists determine the molecular composition of matter.

Basic devices, like scales and rulers, measure the physical properties of matter. Scientists often measure the size, volume, and mass of different forms of matter.

Thermometers and calorimeters measure the energy exchanged in chemical reactions. Temperature change during chemical reactions is indicative of the flow of energy into or out of a system of reactants and products.

Skill 4.2   Describe the nature of chemical changes in matter

Chemical formulas

Aerobic respiration: Let us look at this example. Our tissues need energy for growth, repair, movement, excretion, and so on. This energy is obtained from glucose supplied to the tissues by our blood. In aerobic respiration, glucose is broken down in the presence of oxygen into carbon dioxide and water and energy is released, which is used for our metabolic processes.
The above reaction can be written in the form of a word reaction:

Glucose + Oxygen = Carbon Dioxide + Water + Energy

By using chemical symbols and subscripts we can rewrite the above word equation into a proper chemical equation:

$C_6H_{12}O_6 + 6 O_2 = 6 CO_2 + 6 H_2O + Energy$

Reactions

There are four kinds of chemical reactions:

In a **composition reaction**, two or more substances combine to form a compound.

$A + B \rightarrow AB$
i.e. silver and sulfur yield silver dioxide

In a **decomposition reaction**, a compound breaks down into two or more simpler substances.

$AB \rightarrow A + B$
i.e. water breaks down into hydrogen and oxygen

In a **single replacement reaction**, a free element replaces an element that is part of a compound.

$A + BX \rightarrow AX + B$
i.e. iron plus copper sulfate yields iron sulfate plus copper

In a **double replacement reaction**, parts of two compounds replace each other. In this case, the compounds seem to switch partners.

$AX + BY \rightarrow AY + BX$
i.e. sodium chloride plus mercury nitrate yields sodium nitrate plus mercury chloride

Bonding

The outermost electrons in the atoms are called **valence electrons.** Because they are the ones involved in the bonding process, they determine the properties of the element.

A **chemical bond** is a force of attraction that holds atoms together. When atoms are bonded chemically, they cease to have their individual properties. For instance, hydrogen and oxygen combine into water and no longer look like hydrogen and oxygen. They look like water.

A **covalent bond** is formed when two atoms share electrons. Recall that atoms whose outer shells are not filled with electrons are unstable. When they are unstable, they readily combine with other unstable atoms. By combining and sharing electrons, they act as a single unit. Covalent bonding happens among nonmetals. Covalent bonds are always polar when between two non-identical atoms.

Covalent compounds are compounds whose atoms are joined by covalent bonds. Table sugar, methane, and ammonia are examples of covalent compounds.

An **ionic bond** is a bond formed by the transfer of electrons. It happens when metals and nonmetals bond. Before chlorine and sodium combine, the sodium has one valence electron and chlorine has seven. Neither valence shell is filled, but the chlorine's valence shell is almost full. During the reaction, the sodium gives one valence electron to the chlorine atom. Both atoms then have filled shells and are stable. Something else has happened during the bonding. Before the bonding, both atoms were neutral. When one electron was transferred, it upset the balance of protons and electrons in each atom. The chlorine atom took on one extra electron and the sodium atom released one atom. The atoms have now become ions. **Ions** are atoms with an unequal number of protons and electrons. To determine whether the ion is positive or negative, compare the number of protons (+charge) to the electrons (-charge). If there are more electrons the ion will be negative. If there are more protons, the ion will be positive.

Compounds that result from the transfer of metal atoms to nonmetal atoms are called **ionic compounds.** Sodium chloride (table salt), sodium hydroxide (drain cleaner), and potassium chloride (salt substitute) are examples of ionic compounds.

Spontaneous diffusion occurs when random motion leads particles to increase entropy by equalizing concentrations. Particles tend to move into places of lower concentration. For example, water will move into a cell if the concentration is greater outside than inside the cell. Spontaneous diffusion keeps cells balanced.

Metallic bonding exists only in metals, such as aluminum, gold, copper, and iron. In metals, each atom is bonded to several other metal atoms, and their electrons are free to move throughout the metal structure. This special situation is responsible for the unique properties of metals, such as their high conductivity. For example, a piece of copper metal has a certain arrangement of copper atoms. The valence electrons of these atoms are free to move about the piece of metal and are attracted to the positive cores of copper, thus holding the atoms together. The model that tends to be applied is Band Theory but for now we can imagine the metal ions held together by this "sea" of electrons. This allows the metal to be bent and distorted without the structure breaking.

Hydrogen bonding is an example of dipole-dipole interaction. An everyday example of this is in water. The oxygen-hydrogen bond is polar, oxygen being the more electronegative element. The molecule is therefore polar (the molecule is not linear but has a bent, V shape). This is extenuated by the two lone pairs of electrons on the oxygen atom. One end of the molecule is partially negative while the two hydrogen atoms become partially positive. The molecules of water are attracted to one another, with the slightly positive hydrogens attracted to the negative "ends" (the oxygens) of other water molecules. This intermolecular attraction is termed "hydrogen bonding", and acts almost like a glue holding the molecules of water together. In the case of water the effect on the physical properties of water are quite astounding. The boiling point of water, for example, is much greater than would be the case if such bonding did not exist. This fact alone should make the human race (and the rest of life) grateful for hydrogen bonding since water would otherwise be a gas at room temperature. Further, hydrogen bonds can occur within and between other molecules. For instance, the two strands of a DNA molecule are held together by hydrogen bonds. Hydrogen bonding between water molecules and the amino acids of proteins are involved in maintaining the protein's proper shape.

Rate of Reaction

Reaction rates vary widely according to conditions. A reaction where the reactants and products are stable is said to have reached equilibrium. Prior to reaching equilibrium, the reaction can proceed either forward or backward. The most common sources of disturbance for reactions are temperature, pressure, pH, concentration, and the presence of an inhibitor or catalyst. In addition, enzymes act as biological catalysts to speed up reactions.

Skill 4.3   Describe the nature of physical changes in matter

A **physical change** does not create a new substance. **Atoms are not rearranged into different compounds**. The material has the same chemical composition as it had before the change. Changes of state as described in the previous section are physical changes. Frozen water or gaseous water is still H_2O. Taking a piece of paper and tearing it up is a physical change. You simply have smaller pieces of paper.

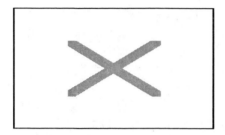

Compare these two nails....They are still iron nails, made of iron atoms. The difference is that one is bent while the other is straight. This is a physical change.

A **chemical change** is a chemical reaction. It **converts one substance into another** because atoms are rearranged to form a different compound. Paper undergoes a chemical change when you burn it. You no longer have paper. A chemical change to a pure substance alters its properties.

An iron nail rusts to form a rusty nail. The rusty nail, however, is not made up of the same iron atoms. It is now composed of iron (III) oxide molecules that form when the iron atoms combine with oxygen molecules during oxidation (rusting).

Changes in State

The kinetic theory states that matter consists of molecules, possessing kinetic energies, in continual random motion. The state of matter (solid, liquid, or gas) depends on the speed of the molecules and the amount of kinetic energy the molecules possess. The molecules of solid matter merely vibrate allowing strong intermolecular forces to hold the molecules in place. The molecules of liquid matter move freely and quickly throughout the body and the molecules of gaseous matter move randomly and at high speeds.

Matter changes state when energy is added or taken away. The addition of energy, usually in the form of heat, increases the speed and kinetic energy of the component molecules. Faster moving molecules more readily overcome the intermolecular attractions that maintain the form of solids and liquids. In conclusion, as the speed of molecules increases, matter changes state from solid to liquid to gas (melting and evaporation).

As matter loses heat energy to the environment, the speed of the component molecules decrease. Intermolecular forces have greater impact on slower moving molecules. Thus, as the speed of molecules decrease, matter changes from gas to liquid to solid (condensation and freezing).

Mass

Everything in our world is made up of **matter**, whether it is a rock, a building, an animal, or a person. Matter is defined by its characteristics: It takes up space and it has mass.

Mass is a measure of the amount of matter in an object. Two objects of equal mass will balance each other on a simple balance scale no matter where the scale is located. For instance, two rocks with the same amount of mass that are in balance on earth will also be in balance on the moon. They will feel heavier on earth than on the moon because of the gravitational pull of the earth. So, although the two rocks have the same mass, they will have different **weight.**

Weight is the measure of the earth's pull of gravity on an object. It can also be defined as the pull of gravity between other bodies. The units of weight measure that we commonly use are the pound in English measure and the kilogram in metric measure.

Conservation of Mass

The principle of conservation states that certain measurable properties of an isolated system remain constant despite changes in the system. Two important principles of conservation are the conservation of mass and charge.

The principle of conservation of mass states that the total mass of a system is constant. Examples of conservation in mass in nature include the burning of wood, rusting of iron, and phase changes of matter. When wood burns, the total mass of the products, such as soot, ash, and gases, equals the mass of the wood and the oxygen that reacts with it. When iron reacts with oxygen, rust forms. The total mass of the iron-rust complex does not change. Finally, when matter changes phase, mass remains constant. Thus, when a glacier melts due to atmospheric warming, the mass of liquid water formed is equal to the mass of the glacier.

Mixtures and Solutions

The two main classes of matter are **pure substances and mixtures.** Each of these classes can also be divided into smaller categories such as elements, compounds, homogeneous mixtures or heterogeneous mixtures based on composition.

Pure Substances: A pure substance is a form of matter with a definite composition and distinct properties. This type of matter can not be separated by ordinary processes like filtering, centrifuging, boiling or melting.
Pure substances are divided into elements and compounds.
Elements: A single type of matter, called an atom, is present. Elements can not be broken down any farther by ordinary chemical processes. They are the smallest whole part of a substance that still represents that substance.
Compounds: Two or more elements chemically combined are present. A compound may be broken down into its elements by chemical processes such as heating or electric current. Compounds have a uniform composition regardless of the sample size or source of the sample.

MIXTURES: Two or more pure substances that are not chemically combined are present. Mixtures may be of any proportion and can be physically separated by processes like filtering, centrifuging, boiling or melting. Mixtures can be classified according to particle size.

SOLUTIONS: Are also known as homogeneous mixtures. They have the same composition and properties throughout the mixture. They have a uniform color and distribution of solute and solvent particles throughout the mixture.

Skill 4.4   Apply knowledge of the kinetic molecular model to explain observable phenomena

Gas **pressure** results from molecular collisions with container walls. The **number of molecules** striking an **area** on the walls and the **average kinetic energy** per molecule are the only factors that contribute to pressure. A higher **temperature** increases speed and kinetic energy. There are more collisions at higher temperatures, but the average distance between molecules does not change, and thus density does not change in a sealed container.

Kinetic molecular theory (KMT)explains how the pressure and temperature influences behavior of gases by making a few assumptions, namely:

1) The energies of intermolecular attractive and repulsive forces may be neglected.
2) The average kinetic energy of the molecules is proportional to absolute temperature.
3) Energy can be transferred between molecules during collisions and the collisions are elastic, so the average kinetic energy of the molecules doesn't change due to collisions.
4) The volume of all molecules in a gas is negligible compared to the total volume of the container.

Strictly speaking, molecules also contain some kinetic energy by rotating or experiencing other motions. The motion of a molecule from one place to another is called **translation**. Translational kinetic energy is the form that is transferred by collisions, and kinetic molecular theory ignores other forms of kinetic energy because they are not proportional to temperature.

Molecules have **kinetic energy (**they move around), and they also have **intermolecular attractive forces** (they stick to each other). The relationship between these two determines whether a collection of molecules will be a gas, liquid, or solid.

A **gas** has an indefinite shape and an indefinite volume. The kinetic model for a gas is a collection of widely separated molecules, each moving in a random and free fashion, with negligible attractive or repulsive forces between them. Gases will expand to occupy a larger container so there is more space between the molecules. Gases can also be compressed to fit into a small container so the molecules are less separated. **Diffusion** occurs when one material spreads into or through another. Gases diffuse rapidly and move from one place to another.

A **liquid** assumes the shape of the portion of any container that it occupies and has a specific volume. The kinetic model for a liquid is a collection of molecules attracted to each other with sufficient strength to keep them close to each other but with insufficient strength to prevent them from moving around randomly. Liquids have a higher density and are much less compressible than gases because the molecules in a liquid are closer together. Diffusion occurs more slowly in liquids than in gases because the molecules in a liquid stick to each other and are not completely free to move.

A **solid** has a definite volume and definite shape. The kinetic model for a solid is a collection of molecules attracted to each other with sufficient strength to essentially lock them in place. Each molecule may vibrate, but it has an average position relative to its neighbors. If these positions form an ordered pattern, the solid is called **crystalline**. Otherwise, it is called **amorphous**. Solids have a high density and are almost incompressible because the molecules are close together. Diffusion occurs extremely slowly because the molecules almost never alter their position.

In a solid, the energy of intermolecular attractive forces is much stronger than the kinetic energy of the molecules, so kinetic energy and kinetic molecular theory are not very important. As temperature increases in a solid, the vibrations of individual molecules grow more intense and the molecules spread slightly further apart, decreasing the density of the solid.

In a liquid, the energy of intermolecular attractive forces is about as strong as the kinetic energy of the molecules and both play a role in the properties of liquids.

In a gas, the energy of intermolecular forces is much weaker than the kinetic energy of the molecules. Kinetic molecular theory is usually applied for gases and is best applied by imagining ourselves shrinking down to become a molecule and picturing what happens when we bump into other molecules and into container walls.

Skill 4.5   Explain the basic concepts of force, work, power, and motion as applied in real world contexts

Dynamics is the study of the relationship between motion and the forces affecting motion. **Force** causes motion. Types of force include:

Push and pulls –Pushing a volleyball or pulling a bowstring applies muscular force when the muscles expand and contract. When the bowstring is released it is elastic force and the object returns to its original shape.

Rubbing – Friction opposes the motion of one surface past another. Friction is common when slowing down a car.

Pull of gravity – is a force of attraction between two objects. Gravity questions can be raised not only on earth but also between planets and even black hole discussions.

Forces on objects at rest – The formula F= m/a means that a force equals mass over acceleration. An object will not move unless the force is strong enough to move the mass. Also there can be opposing forces holding the object in place. For instance a boat may want to be forced by the currents to drift away but an equal and opposite force is a rope holding it to a dock.

Forces on a moving object - Overcoming inertia is the tendency of any object to oppose a change in motion. An object at rest tends to stay at rest. An object that is moving tends to keep moving.

Inertia and circular motion – The centripetal force is provided by the high banking of the curved road and by friction between the wheels and the road. This inward force that keeps an object moving in a circle is centripetal force.

Energy and Work

Whenever work is done upon an object by an external force, there will be a change in the total mechanical energy of the object. If only internal forces are doing work (no work done by external forces), there is no change in total mechanical energy, the total mechanical energy is "conserved." The quantitative relationship between work and mechanical energy is expressed by the following equation:

$$TME_i + W_{ext} = TME_f$$

The equation states that the initial amount of total mechanical energy (TME_i) plus the work done by external forces (W_{ext}) is equal to the final amount of total mechanical energy (TME_f).

Power

Power is the rate at which work is done. It is the work/time ratio. The following equation is the formula used to compute power:

$$Power = \frac{Work}{Time}$$

The standard metric unit of power is the Watt. A unit of power is equivalent to a unit of work divided by a unit of time. Therefore, a Watt is equivalent to a Joule/second.

Mechanical Advantage

There are two types of mechanical advantage, ideal and actual. Ideal mechanical advantage is the mechanical advantage of an ideal machine. Because such a machine does not really exist, we use physics principals to "theoretically" solve such equations. The ideal mechanical advantage (IMA) is found using the following formula:

$$IMA = D_E / D_R$$

The effort distance over the resistance distance gives us the IMA.

Actual mechanical advantage it the mechanical advantage of a real machine and takes into consideration factors such as energy lost to friction. Actual mechanical advantage (AMA) is calculated using the following formula:

$$AMA = R / E_{actual}$$

By dividing the resistance force by the actual effort force, we can determine the actual mechanical advantage of a machine.

Efficiency is the relationship between energy input and energy output. Efficiency is expressed as a percentage. The more efficient a system is, the less energy that is lost within that system. The percentage efficiency of any machine can be calculated as long as you know how much energy has to be put into the machine and how much useful energy comes out. The following equation is used:

$$\% \text{ efficiency} = \frac{\text{useful energy produced}}{\text{total energy used}} \times 100$$

Simple machines are used to make work easier. The most common are:

1. Inclined plane
2. Lever
3. Wheel and axle
4. Pulley

Distance is a scalar quantity that refers to how much ground an object has covered while moving. **Displacement** is a vector quantity that refers to the object's change in position.

Example:

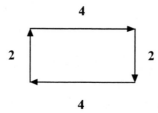

Jamie walked 2 miles north, 4 miles east, 2 miles south, and then 4 miles west. In terms of distance, she walked 12 miles. However, there is no displacement because the directions cancelled each other out, and she returned to her starting position.

Speed is a scalar quantity that refers to how fast an object is moving (ex. the car was traveling 60 mi/hr). **Velocity** is a vector quantity that refers to the rate at which an object changes its position. In other words, velocity is speed with direction (ex. the car was traveling 60 mi/hr east).

$$\text{Average speed} = \frac{\text{Distance traveled}}{\text{Time of travel}}$$

$$v = \frac{d}{t}$$

$$\text{Average velocity} = \frac{\triangle \text{position}}{\text{time}} = \frac{\text{displacement}}{\text{time}}$$

Instantaneous Speed - speed at any given instant in time.

Average Speed - average of all instantaneous speeds, found simply by a distance/time ratio.

Acceleration is a vector quantity defined as the rate at which an object changes its velocity.

$$a = \frac{\triangle velocity}{time} = \frac{v_f - v_i}{t}$$ where *f* represents the final velocity and *i* represents the initial velocity

Since acceleration is a vector quantity, it always has a direction associated with it. The direction of the acceleration vector depends on

- whether the object is speeding up or slowing down
- whether the object is moving in the positive or negative direction.

Skill 4.6   Describe energy and the forms that it can take

The law of conservation of energy states that energy is neither created nor destroyed. Thus, energy changes form when energy transactions occur in nature. The following are the major forms energy can take.

Thermal energy is the total internal energy of objects created by the vibration and movement of atoms and molecules. Heat is the transfer of thermal energy.

Acoustical energy, or sound energy, is the movement of energy through an object in waves. Energy that forces an object to vibrate creates sound.

Radiant energy is the energy of electromagnetic waves. Visible light and UV light are examples of radiant energy.

Electrical energy is the movement of electrical charges in an electromagnetic field. Examples of electrical energy are electricity and lightning.

Chemical energy is the energy stored in the chemical bonds of molecules. For example, the energy derived from gasoline is chemical energy.

Mechanical energy is the potential and kinetic energy of a mechanical system. Rolling balls, car engines, and body parts in motion exemplify mechanical energy.

Nuclear energy is the energy present in the nucleus of atoms. Division, combination, or collision of nuclei release nuclear energy.

Energy Transfer

Thermodynamics is the study of energy and energy transfer. The First Law of Thermodynamics states the energy of the universe is constant. Thus, interactions involving energy deal with the transfer and transformation of energy, not the creation or destruction of energy.

Electricity is an important source of energy. Ovens and electric heaters convert electrical energy into heat energy. Electrical energy energizes the filament of a light bulb to produce light. Finally, the movement of electrical charges creates magnetic fields. Charges moving in a magnetic field experience a force, which is a transfer of energy.

The process of photosynthesis converts light energy from the sun into chemical energy (sugar). Cellular respiration later converts the sugar into ATP, a major energy source of all living organisms. Plants and certain types of bacteria carry out photosynthesis. The actions of the green pigment chlorophyll allow the conversion of unusable light energy into usable chemical energy.

Energy transfer plays an important role in weather processes. The three main types of heat transfer to the atmosphere are radiation, conduction, and convection. Radiation is the transfer of heat by electromagnetic waves. Sunlight is an example of radiation. Conduction is the transfer of energy from one substance to another, or within a substance. Convection is the transfer of heat energy in a fluid. Air in the atmosphere acts as a fluid for the transfer of heat energy. Convection, resulting indirectly from the energy generated by sunlight, is responsible for many weather phenomena including wind and clouds.

Kinetic and Potential Energies

Mechanical energy is the potential and kinetic energy of a mechanical system. Rolling balls, car engines, and body parts in motion exemplify mechanical energy. Interacting objects in the universe constantly exchange and transform energy. Total energy remains the same, but the form of the energy readily changes. Energy often changes from kinetic (motion) to potential (stored) or potential to kinetic.

Skill 4.7   Analyze the characteristics and behavior of waves, sound, and light

Spectrum

Light, microwaves, x-rays, and TV and radio transmissions are all kinds of electromagnetic waves. They are all a wavy disturbance that repeats itself over a distance called the wavelength. Electromagnetic waves come in varying sizes and properties, by which they are organized in the electromagnetic spectrum. The electromagnetic spectrum is measured in frequency (f) in hertz and wavelength (λ) in meters. The frequency times the wavelength of every electromagnetic wave equals the speed of light (3.0 x 109 meters/second).

Roughly, the range of wavelengths of the electromagnetic spectrum is:

	λ		f	
Radio waves	$10^{5} - 10^{-1}$	meters	$10^{3} - 10^{9}$	hertz
Microwaves	$10^{-1} - 10^{-3}$	meters	$10^{9} - 10^{11}$	hertz
Infrared radiation	$10^{-3} - 10^{-6}$	meters	$10^{11.2} - 10^{14.3}$	hertz
Visible light	$10^{-6.2} - 10^{-6.9}$	meters	$10^{14.3} - 10^{15}$	hertz
Ultraviolet radiation	$10^{-7} - 10^{-9}$	meters	$10^{15} - 10^{17.2}$	hertz
X-Rays	$10^{-9} - 10^{-11}$	meters	$10^{17.2} - 10^{19}$	hertz
Gamma Rays	$10^{-11} - 10^{-15}$	meters	$10^{19} - 10^{23}$	hertz

Radio waves are used for transmitting data. Common examples are television, cell phones, and wireless computer networks. Microwaves are used to heat food and deliver Wi-Fi service. Infrared waves are utilized in night vision goggles. We are all familiar with visible light as the human eye is most sensitive to this wavelength range. UV light causes sunburns and would be even more harmful if most of it were not captured in the Earth's ozone layer. X-rays aid us in the medical field and gamma rays are most useful in the field of astronomy.

Waves

Transverse waves are characterized by the particle motion being perpendicular to the wave motion; **longitudinal waves** are characterized by the particle motion being parallel to the wave motion.

Transverse Wave

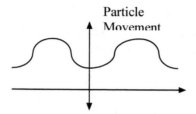

Direction of Energy Transport

Longitudinal Wave

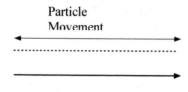

Direction of Energy Transport

Transverse waves cannot spread in a gas or liquid. Sound waves are a good example of longitudinal waves.

Wave Terminology

The **pitch** of a sound depends on the **frequency** that the ear receives. High-pitched sound waves have high frequencies. High notes are produced by an object that is vibrating at a greater number of times per second than one that produces a low note.

The **intensity** of a sound is the amount of energy that crosses a unit of area in a given unit of time. The loudness of the sound is subjective and depends upon the effect on the human ear. Two tones of the same intensity but different pitches may appear to have different loudness. The intensity level of sound is measured in decibels. Normal conversation is about 60 decibels. A power saw is about 110 decibels.

The **amplitude** of a sound wave determines its loudness. Loud sound waves have large amplitudes. The larger the sound wave, the more energy is needed to create the wave.

The **wavelength** is the distance measured between repeating units of a wave pattern. It is written as λ and has an inverse relationship to frequency. The wavelength is equal to the speed of the wave type divided by the frequency of the wave.

Frequency, abbreviated f, is the number of peaks to pass a single point in a given time.

Wave **interference** occurs when two waves meet while traveling along the same medium. The medium takes on a shape resulting from the net effect of the individual waves upon the particles of the medium. There are two types of interference: constructive and destructive.

Constructive interference occurs when two crests or two troughs of the same shape meet. The medium will take on the shape of a crest or a trough with twice the amplitude of the two interfering crests or troughs. If a trough and a crest of the same shape meet, the two pulses will cancel each other out, and the medium will assume the equilibrium position. This is called **destructive** interference.

Destructive interference in sound waves will reduce the loudness of the sound. This is a disadvantage in rooms, such as auditoriums, where sound needs to be at its optimum. However, it can be used as an advantage in noise reduction systems. When two sound waves differing slightly in frequency are superimposed, beats are created by the alternation of constructive and destructive interference. The frequency of the beats is equal to the difference between the frequencies of the interfering sound waves.

Wave interference occurs with light waves in much the same manner that it does with sound waves. If two light waves of the same color, frequency, and amplitude are combined, the interference shows up as fringes of alternating light and dark bands. In order for this to happen, the light waves must come from the same source.

Wave Behavior

The place where one medium ends and another begins is called a **boundary**, and the manner in which a wave behaves when it reaches that boundary is called **boundary behavior**. The following principles apply to boundary behavior in waves:

1. Wave speed is always greater in the less dense medium
2. Wavelength is always greater in the less dense medium
3. Wave frequency is not changed by crossing a boundary
4. The reflected pulse becomes inverted when a wave in a less dense medium is heading towards a boundary with a more dense medium
5. The amplitude of the incident pulse is always greater than the amplitude of the reflected pulse.

Reflection occurs when waves bounce off a barrier. The **law of reflection** states that when a ray of light reflects off a surface, the angle of incidence is equal to the angle of reflection.

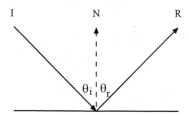

Line I represents the **incident ray**, the ray of light striking the surface. Line R is the **reflected ray**, the ray of light reflected off the surface. Line N is known as the **normal line**. It is a perpendicular line at the point of incidence that divides the angle between the incident ray and the reflected ray into two equal rays. The angle between the incident ray and the normal line is called the **angle of incidence**; the angle between the reflected ray and the normal line is called the **angle of reflection**.

Waves passing from one medium into another will undergo **refraction**, or bending. Accompanying this bending are a change in both speed and the wavelength of the waves.

In this example, light waves traveling through the air will pass through glass.

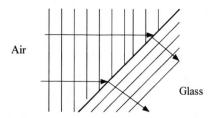

Refraction occurs only at the boundary. Once the wavefront passes across the boundary, it travels in a straight line.

Diffraction involves a change in direction of waves as they pass through an opening or around an obstacle in their path.

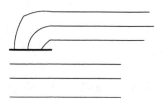

The amount of diffraction depends upon the wavelength. The amount of diffraction increases with increasing wavelength and decreases with decreasing wavelength. Sound and water waves exhibit this ability.

Phenomena

The amount of diffraction depends upon the wavelength. The amount of diffraction increases with increasing wavelength and decreases with decreasing wavelength. Sound and water waves exhibit this ability.

When we refer to light, we are usually talking about a type of electromagnetic wave that stimulates the retina of the eye, or visible light. Each individual wavelength within the spectrum of visible light represents a particular **color**. When a particular wavelength strikes the retina, we perceive that color. Visible light is sometimes referred to as ROYGBIV (red, orange, yellow, green, blue, indigo, violet). The visible light spectrum ranges from red (the longest wavelength) to violet (the shortest wavelength) with a range of wavelengths in between. If all the wavelengths strike your eye at the same time, you will see white. Conversely, when no wavelengths strike your eye, you perceive black.

A **shadow** results from the inability of light waves to diffract as sound and water waves can. An obstacle in the way of the light waves blocks the light waves, thereby creating a shadow.

Mirrors reflect images because when hit by photons (particles of light), they reflect the photons back to us and some of the photons reach, and enter, our eyes. Photons that hit a smooth surface, such as a mirror, only bounce off the surface at the same angle at which they hit the object.

Skill 4.8   Describe electricity, magnets, and electromagnetism.

Electrostatics is the study of stationary electric charges. A plastic rod that is rubbed with fur or a glass rod that is rubbed with silk will become electrically charged and will attract small pieces of paper. The charge on the plastic rod rubbed with fur is negative and the charge on glass rod rubbed with silk is positive.

Electrically charged objects share these characteristics:

1. Like charges repel one another.
2. Opposite charges attract each other.
3. Charge is conserved. A neutral object has no net change. If the plastic rod and fur are initially neutral, when the rod becomes charged by the fur a negative charge is transferred from the fur to the rod. The net negative charge on the rod is equal to the net positive charge on the fur.

Materials through which electric charges can easily flow are called conductors. On the other hand, an **insulator** is a material through which electric charges do not move easily, if at all. A simple device used to indicate the existence of a positive or negative charge is called an **electroscope**. An electroscope is made up of a conducting knob and attached very lightweight conducting leaves - usually made of gold foil or aluminum foil. When a charged object touches the knob, the leaves push away from each other because like charges repel. It is not possible to tell whether or not the charge is positive or negative.

Charging by induction:

Touch the knob with a finger while a charged rod is nearby. The electrons will be repulsed and flow out of the electroscope through the hand. If the hand is removed while the charged rod remains close, the electroscope will retain the charge.

When an object is rubbed with a charged rod, the object will take on the same charge as the rod. However, charging by induction gives the object the opposite charge as that of the charged rod.

Grounding charge:

Charge can be removed from an object by connecting it to the earth through a conductor. The removal of static electricity by conduction is called **grounding**.

Circuits

An **electric circuit** is a path along which electrons flow. A simple circuit can be created with a dry cell, wire, and a bell, or light bulb. When all are connected, the electrons flow from the negative terminal, through the wire to the device and back to the positive terminal of the dry cell. If there are no breaks in the circuit, the device will work. The circuit is closed. Any break in the flow will create an open circuit and cause the device to shut off.

The device (bell, bulb) is an example of a **load**. A load is a device that uses energy. Suppose that you also add a buzzer so that the bell rings when you press the buzzer button. The buzzer is acting as a **switch**. A switch is a device that opens or closes a circuit. Pressing the buzzer makes the connection complete and the bell rings. When the buzzer is not engaged, the circuit is open and the bell is silent.

A **series circuit** is one where the electrons have only one path along which they can move. When one load in a series circuit goes out, the circuit is open. An example of this is a set of Christmas tree lights that is missing a bulb. None of the bulbs will work.

A **parallel circuit** is one where the electrons have more than one path to move along. Each path is known as a path. If a load goes out in a parallel circuit, the other load will still work because the electrons can still find a way to continue moving along the path.

When an electron goes through a load, it does work and therefore loses some of its energy. The measure of how much energy is lost is called the **potential difference**. The potential difference between two points is the work needed to move a charge from one point to another.

Potential difference is measured in a unit called the volt. **Voltage** is potential difference. The higher the voltage, the more energy the electrons have. This energy is measured by a device called a voltmeter. To use a voltmeter, place it in a circuit parallel with the load you are measuring.

Current is the number of electrons per second that flow past a point in a circuit. Current is measured with a device called an ammeter. To use an ammeter, put it in series with the load you are measuring.

As electrons flow through a wire, they lose potential energy. Some is changed into heat energy because of resistance. **Resistance** is the ability of the material to oppose the flow of electrons through it. All substances have some resistance, even if they are a good conductor such as copper. This resistance is measured in units called **ohms**. A thin wire will have more resistance than a thick one because it will have less room for electrons to travel. In a thicker wire, there will be more possible paths for the electrons to flow. Resistance also depends upon the length of the wire. The longer the wire, the more resistance it will have. Potential difference, resistance, and current form a relationship know as **Ohm's Law**. Current **(I)** is equal to potential difference **(V)** divided by resistance **(R)**.

$$I = V / R$$

If you have a wire with resistance of 5 ohms and a potential difference of 75 volts, you can calculate the current by

I = 75 volts / 5 ohms
I = 15 amperes

A current of 10 or more amperes will cause a wire to get hot. 22 amperes is about the maximum for a house circuit. Anything above 25 amperes can start a fire.

Magnetism

Magnets have a north pole and a south pole. Like poles repel and different poles attract. A **magnetic field** is the space around a magnet where its force will affect objects. The closer you are to a magnet, the stronger the force. As you move away, the force becomes weaker.

Some materials act as magnets and some do not. This is because magnetism is a result of electrons in motion. The most important motion in this case is the spinning of the individual electrons. Electrons spin in pairs in opposite directions in most atoms. Each spinning electron has the magnetic field that it creates canceled out by the electron that is spinning in the opposite direction.

In an atom of iron, there are four unpaired electrons. The magnetic fields of these are not canceled out. Their fields add up to make a tiny magnet. The fields exert forces on each other setting up small areas in the iron called **magnetic domains** where atomic magnetic fields line up in the same direction.

You can make a magnet out of an iron nail by stroking the nail in the same direction repeatedly with a magnet. This causes poles in the atomic magnets in the nail to be attracted to the magnet. The tiny magnetic fields in the nail line up in the direction of the magnet. The magnet causes the domains pointing in its direction in the nail to grow. Eventually, one large domain results and the nail becomes a magnet.

A bar magnet has a north pole and a south pole. If you break the magnet in half, each piece will have a north and south pole.

The earth has a magnetic field. In a compass, a tiny, lightweight magnet is suspended and will line its south pole up with the North Pole magnet of the earth.

A magnet can be made out of a coil of wire by connecting the ends of the coil to a battery. When the current goes through the wire, the wire acts in the same way that a magnet does, it is called an **electromagnet**.

The poles of the electromagnet will depend upon which way the electric current runs. An electromagnet can be made more powerful in three ways:

1. Make more coils.
2. Put an iron core (nail) inside the coils.
3. Use more battery power.

Everyday applications

Telegraphs use electromagnets to work. When a telegraph key is pushed, current flows through a circuit, turning on an electromagnet which attracts an iron bar. The iron bar hits a sounding board which responds with a click. Release the key and the electromagnet turns off. Messages can be sent around the world in this way.

Scrap metal can be removed from waste materials by the use of a large electromagnet that is suspended from a crane. When the electromagnet is turned on, the metal in the pile of waste will be attracted to it. All other materials will stay on the ground.

Air conditioners, vacuum cleaners, and washing machines use electric motors. An electric motor uses an electromagnet to change electrical energy into mechanical energy.

COMPETENCY 5.0   USING KNOWLEDGE OF EARTH AND SPACE SCIENCE

Skill 5.1   Apply knowledge of geologic history and processes to the changing earth

Origin of Earth

Two main theories to explain the origins of the universe include: (1) **The Big Bang Theory** and (2) **The Steady-State Theory.**

The Steady-State Theory is the least accepted theory. It states that the universe is continuously being renewed. Galaxies move outward and new galaxies replace the older galaxies. Astronomers have not found any evidence to prove this theory.

The dominant scientific theory about the origin of the Universe, and consequently the Earth, is the **Big Bang Theory**. According to this theory, a point source exploded about 10 to 20 billion years ago throwing matter in all directions. Although this theory has never been proven, and probably never will be, it is supported by the fact that distant galaxies in every direction are moving away from us at great speeds.

Earth, itself, is believed to have been created 4.5 billion years ago as a solidified cloud of gases and dust left over from the creation of the sun. As millions of years passed, radioactive decay released energy that melted some of Earth's components. Over time, the heavier components sank to the center of the Earth and accumulated into the core. As the Earth cooled, a crust formed with natural depressions. Water rising from the interior of the Earth filled these depressions and formed the oceans. Slowly, the Earth acquired the appearance it has today.

Geology

Earth's history extends over more than four billion years and is reckoned in terms of a scale. Paleontologists who study the history of the Earth have divided this huge period of time into four large time units called eons. Eons are divided into smaller units of time called eras. An era refers to a time interval in which particular plants and animals were dominant, or present in great abundance. The end of an era is most often characterized by (1) a general uplifting of the crust, (2) the extinction of the dominant plants or animals, and (3) the appearance of new life-forms.

Each era is divided into several smaller divisions of time called periods. Some periods are divided into smaller time units called epochs.

Estimates of the Earth's age have been made possible with the discovery of Radioactivity and the invention of instruments that can measure the amount of radioactivity in rocks. The use of radioactivity to make accurate determinations of Earth's age, is called Absolute Dating. This process depends upon comparing the amount of radioactive material in a rock with the amount that has decayed into another element. Studying the radiations given off by atoms of radioactive elements is the most accurate method of measuring the Earth's age. These atoms are unstable and are continuously breaking down or undergoing decay. The radioactive element that decays is called the parent element. The new element that results from the radioactive decay of the parent element is called the daughter element.

The time required for one half of a given amount of a radioactive element to decay is called the half-life of that element or compound. Geologists commonly use Carbon Dating to calculate the age of a fossil substance.

Earth's interior

The interior of the Earth is divided in to three chemically distinct layers. Starting from the middle and moving towards the surface, these are: the core, the mantle, and the crust. Much of what we know about the inner structure of the Earth has been inferred from various data. Subsequently, there is still some uncertainty about the composition and conditions in the Earth's interior.

Core

The outer core of the Earth begins about 3000 km beneath the surface and is a liquid, though far more viscous than that of the mantle. Even deeper, approximately 5000 beneath the surface, is the solid inner core. The inner core has a radius of about 1200 km. Temperatures in the core exceed 4000°C. Scientists agree that the core is extremely dense. This conclusion is based on the fact that the Earth is known to have an average density of 5515 kg/m^3 even though the material close to the surface has an average density of only 3000 kg/m^3. Therefore a denser core must exist. Additionally, it is hypothesized that when the Earth was forming, the densest material sank to the middle of the planet. Thus, it is not surprising that the core is about 80% iron. In fact, there is some speculation that the entire inner core is a single iron crystal, while the outer core is a mix of liquid iron and nickel.

Mantle

The Earth's mantle begins about 35 km beneath the surface and stretches all the way to 3000 km beneath the surface, where the outer core begins. Since the mantle stretches so far into the Earth's center, its temperature varies widely; near the boundary with the crust it is approximately 1000°C, while near the outer core it may reach nearly 4000°C. Within the mantle there are silicate rocks, which are rich in iron and magnesium. The silicate rocks exist as solids, but the high heat means they are ductile enough to "flow" over long time scales. In general, the mantle is semi-solid/plastic and the viscosity varies as pressures and temperatures change at varying depths.

Crust

It is not clear how long the Earth has actually had a solid crust; most of the rocks are less than 100 million years, though some are 4.4 billion years old. The crust of the earth is the outermost layer and continues down for between 5 and 70 km beneath the surface. Thin areas generally exist under ocean basins (oceanic crust) and thicker crust underlies the continents (continental crust). Oceanic crust is composed largely of iron magnesium silicate rocks, while continental crust is less dense and consists mainly of sodium potassium aluminum silicate rocks. The crust is the least dense layer of the Earth and so is rich in those materials that "floated" during Earth's formation. Additionally, some heavier elements that bound to lighter materials are present in the crust.

Interactions between the Layers

It is not the case that these layers exist as separate entities, with little interaction between them. For instance, it is generally believed that swirling of the iron-rich liquid in the outer core results in the Earth's magnetic field, which is readily apparent on the surface. Heat also moves out from the core to the mantle and crust. The core still retains heat from the formation of the Earth and additional heat is generated by the decay of radioactive isotopes. While most of the heat in our atmosphere comes from sun, radiant heat from the core does warm oceans and other large bodies of water.

There is also a great deal of interaction between the mantle and the crust. The slow convection of rocks in the mantle is responsible for the shifting of tectonic plates on the crust. Matter can also move between the layers as occurs during the rock cycle.

Plate Tectonics

Data obtained from many sources led scientists to develop the theory of plate tectonics. This theory is the most current model that explains not only the movement of the continents, but also the changes in the earth's crust caused by internal forces.

Plates are rigid blocks of earth's crust and upper mantle. These rigid solid blocks make up the lithosphere. The earth's lithosphere is broken into nine large sections and several small ones. These moving slabs are called plates. The major plates are named after the continents they are "transporting."

The plates float on and move with a layer of hot, plastic-like rock in the upper mantle. Geologists believe that the heat currents circulating within the mantle cause this plastic zone of rock to slowly flow, carrying along the overlying crustal plates.

Movement of these crustal plates creates areas where the plates diverge as well as areas where the plates converge. In the Mid-Atlantic is a major area of divergence. Currents of hot mantle rock rise and separate at this point of divergence creating new oceanic crust at the rate of 2 to 10 centimeters per year. Convergence is when the oceanic crust collides with either another oceanic plate or a continental plate. The oceanic crust sinks forming an enormous trench and generating volcanic activity. Convergence also includes continent to continent plate collisions. When two plates slide past one another a transform fault is created.

These movements produce many major features of the earth's surface, such as mountain ranges, volcanoes, and earthquake zones. Most of these features are located at plate boundaries, where the plates interact by spreading apart, pressing together, or sliding past each other. These movements are very slow, averaging only a few centimeters a year.

Boundaries form between spreading plates where the crust is forced apart in a process called rifting. Rifting generally occurs at mid-ocean ridges. Rifting can also take place within a continent, splitting the continent into smaller, landmasses that drift away from each other, thereby forming an ocean basin (Red Sea) between them. As the seafloor spreading takes place, new material is added to the inner edges of the separating plates. In this way, the plates grow larger, and the ocean basin widens. This is the process that broke up the super continent Pangaea and created the Atlantic Ocean.

Boundaries between plates that are colliding are zones of intense crustal activity. When a plate of ocean crust collides with a plate of continental crust, the more dense oceanic plate slides under the lighter continental plate and plunges into the mantle. This process is called **subduction**, and the site where it takes place is called a subduction zone. A subduction zone is usually seen on the sea-floor as a deep depression called a trench.

The crustal movement which is characterized by plates sliding sideways past each other produces a plate boundary characterized by major faults that are capable of unleashing powerful earthquakes. The San Andreas Fault forms such a boundary between the Pacific Plate and the North American Plate.

Topographical features and their creation

Orogeny is the term given to natural mountain building.

A mountain is terrain that has been raised high above the surrounding landscape by volcanic action, or some form of tectonic plate collisions. The plate collisions could be intercontinental or ocean floor collisions with a continental crust (subduction). The physical composition of mountains would include igneous, metamorphic, or sedimentary rocks; some may have rock layers that are tilted or distorted by plate collision forces.

There are many different types of mountains. The physical attributes of a mountain range depends upon the angle at which plate movement thrust layers of rock to the surface. Many mountains (Adirondacks, Southern Rockies) were formed along high angle faults.

Folded mountains (Alps, Himalayas) are produced by the folding of rock layers during their formation. The Himalayas are the highest mountains in the world and contains Mount Everest, which rises almost 9 km above sea level. The Himalayas were formed when India collided with Asia. The movement which created this collision is still in process at the rate of a few centimeters per year.

Fault-block mountains (Utah, Arizona, and New Mexico) are created when plate movement produces tension forces instead of compression forces. The area under tension produces normal faults and rock along these faults is displaced upward.

Dome mountains are formed as magma tries to push up through the crust but fails to break the surface. Dome mountains resemble a huge blister on the earth's surface.

Upwarped mountains (Black Hills of South Dakota) are created in association with a broad arching of the crust. They can also be formed by rock thrust upward along high angle faults.

Volcanic mountains are built up by successive deposits of volcanic materials.

Volcanism is the term given to the movement of magma through the crust and its emergence as lava onto the earth's surface.

An active volcano is one that is presently erupting or building to an eruption. A dormant volcano is one that is between eruptions but still shows signs of internal activity that might lead to an eruption in the future. An extinct volcano is said to be no longer capable of erupting. Most of the world's active volcanoes are found along the rim of the Pacific Ocean, which is also a major earthquake zone. This curving belt of active faults and volcanoes is often called the Ring of Fire.

The world's best known volcanic mountains include: Mount Etna in Italy and Mount Kilimanjaro in Africa. The Hawaiian Islands are actually the tops of a chain of volcanic mountains that rise from the ocean floor.

There are three types of volcanic mountains: shield volcanoes, cinder cones and composite volcanoes.

Shield Volcanoes are associated with quiet eruptions. Lava emerges from the vent or opening in the crater and flows freely out over the earth's surface until it cools and hardens into a layer of igneous rock. A repeated lava flow builds this type of volcano into the largest volcanic mountain. Mauna Loa found in Hawaii, is the largest volcano on earth.

Cinder Cone Volcanoes associated with explosive eruptions as lava is hurled high into the air in a spray of droplets of various sizes. These droplets cool and harden into cinders and particles of ash before falling to the ground. The ash and cinder pile up around the vent to form a steep, cone-shaped hill called the cinder cone. Cinder cone volcanoes are relatively small but may form quite rapidly.

Composite Volcanoes are described as being built by both lava flows and layers of ash and cinders. Mount Fuji in Japan, Mount St. Helens in Washington, USA and Mount Vesuvius in Italy are all famous Composite Volcanoes.

Mechanisms of producing mountains

Mountains are produced by different types of mountain-building processes. Most major mountain ranges are formed by the processes of folding and faulting.

Folded Mountains are produced by folding of rock layers. Crustal movements may press horizontal layers of sedimentary rock together from the sides, squeezing them into wavelike folds. Up-folded sections of rock are called anticlines; down-folded sections of rock are called synclines. The Appalachian Mountains are an example of folded mountains with long ridges and valleys in a series of anticlines and synclines formed by folded rock layers.

Faults are fractures in the earth's crust which have been created by either tension or compression forces transmitted through the crust. These forces are produced by the movement of separate blocks of crust.

Faultings are categorized on the basis of the relative movement between the blocks on both sides of the fault plane. The movement can be horizontal, vertical or oblique.

A dip-slip fault occurs when the movement of the plates is vertical and opposite. The displacement is in the direction of the inclination, or dip, of the fault. Dip-slip faults are classified as normal faults when the rock above the fault plane moves down relative to the rock below.

Reverse faults are created when the rock above the fault plane moves up relative to the rock below. Reverse faults having a very low angle to the horizontal are also referred to as thrust faults.

Faults in which the dominant displacement horizontal movement along the trend or strike (length) of the fault, are called strike-slip faults. When a large strike-slip fault is associated with plate boundaries it is called a transform fault. The San Andreas Fault in California is a well-known transform fault.

Faults that have both vertical and horizontal movement are called oblique-slip faults.

When lava cools, igneous rock is formed. This formation can occur either above ground or below ground.

Intrusive rock includes any igneous rock that was formed below the earth's surface. Batholiths are the largest structures of intrusive type rock and are composed of near granite materials; they are the core of the Sierra Nevada Mountains.

Extrusive rock includes any igneous rock that was formed at the earth's surface.

Dikes are old lava tubes formed when magma entered a vertical fracture and hardened. Sometimes magma squeezes between two rock layers and hardens into a thin horizontal sheet called a sill. A **laccolith** is formed in much the same way as a sill, but the magma that creates a **laccolith** is very thick and does not flow easily. It pools and forces the overlying strata creating an obvious surface dome.

A **caldera** is normally formed by the collapse of the top of a volcano. This collapse can be caused by a massive explosion that destroys the cone and empties most if not all of the magma chamber below the volcano. The cone collapses into the empty magma chamber forming a caldera.

An inactive volcano may have magma solidified in its pipe. This structure, called a volcanic neck, is resistant to erosion and today may be the only visible evidence of the past presence of an active volcano.

When lava cools, igneous rock is formed. This formation can occur either above ground or below ground.

Glaciation

A continental glacier covered a large part of North America during the most recent ice age. Evidence of this glacial coverage remains as abrasive grooves, large boulders from northern environments dropped in southerly locations, glacial troughs created by the rounding out of steep valleys by glacial scouring, and the remains of glacial sources called **cirques** that were created by frost wedging the rock at the bottom of the glacier. Remains of plants and animals found in warm climate that have been discovered in the moraines and outwash plains help to support the theory of periods of warmth during the past ice ages.

The Ice Age began about 2 -3 million years ago. This age saw the advancement and retreat of glacial ice over millions of years. Theories relating to the origin of glacial activity include Plate Tectonics where it can be demonstrated that some continental masses, now in temperate climates, were at one time blanketed by ice and snow. Another theory involves changes in the earth's orbit around the sun, changes in the angle of the earth's axis, and the wobbling of the earth's axis. Support for the validity of this theory has come from deep ocean research that indicates a correlation between climatic sensitive microorganisms and the changes in the earth's orbital status.

About 12,000 years ago, a vast sheet of ice covered a large part of the northern United States. This huge, frozen mass had moved southward from the northern regions of Canada as several large bodies of slow-moving ice, or glaciers. A time period in which glaciers advance over a large portion of a continent is called an ice age. A glacier is a large mass of ice that moves or flows over the land in response to gravity. Glaciers form among high mountains and in other cold regions.

There are two main types of glaciers: valley glaciers and continental glaciers. Erosion by valley glaciers is characteristic of U-shaped erosion. They produce sharp peaked mountains such as the Matterhorn in Switzerland. Erosion by continental glaciers often rides over mountains in their paths leaving smoothed, rounded mountains and ridges.

Catastrophic phenomena

Natural phenomena affect the make up and functioning of ecosystems both directly and indirectly. For example, floods and volcanic eruptions can destroy the fixed portions of an ecosystem, such as plants and microbes. Mobile elements, such as animals, must evacuate or risk injury or death. After a catastrophic event, species of microbes and plants begin to repopulate the ecosystem, beginning a line of secondary succession that eventually leads to the return of higher-level species. Often the area affected by the event returns to something like its original state.

Volcanic eruptions produce large amounts of molten lava and expel large amounts of ash and gas. Molten lava kills and destroys any living organisms it contacts. However, when lava cools and hardens, it provides a rich environment for growth of microbes and plants. Volcanic eruptions also affect ecosystems indirectly. Studies show that the ash and gas released by eruptions can cause a reduction in the area temperature for several years. The volcanic aerosol reflects the Sun's rays and creates clouds that have the same effect. In addition, sulfuric acid released by the volcano suppresses the production of greenhouse gases that damage the ozone layer.

Floods destroy microbes and vegetation and kill or force the evacuation of animals. Only when floodwaters recede can an ecosystem begin to return to normal. Floods, however, also have indirect effects. For example, floods can cause permanent soil erosion and nutrient depletion. Such disruptions of the soil can delay and limit an ecosystem's recovery.

Maps

Decode map symbols

Hachures are depressions or tiny comb-like markings that point inward from the contour line toward the bottom of the depression. A contour line that has hachures is called a depression contour.

A system of imaginary lines has been developed that helps people describe exact locations on Earth. Looking at a globe of Earth, you will see lines drawn on it. The equator is drawn around Earth halfway between the North and South Poles. Latitude is a term used to describe distance in degrees north or south of the equator. Lines of latitude are drawn east and west parallel to the equator. Degrees of latitude range from 0 at the equator to 90 at either the North Pole or South Pole. Lines of latitude are also called parallels.

Lines drawn north and south at right angles to the equator and from pole to pole are called meridians. Longitude is a term used to describe distances in degrees east or west of a $0°$ meridian. The prime meridian is the $0°$ meridian and it passes through Greenwich, England.

Time zones are determined by longitudinal lines. Each time zone represents one hour. Since there are 24 hours in one complete rotation of the Earth, there are 24 international time zones. Each time zone is roughly $15°$ wide. While time zones are based on meridians, they do not strictly follow lines of longitude. Time zone boundaries are subject to political decisions and have been moved around cities and other areas at the whim of the electorate.

The International Date Line is the $180°$ meridian and it is on the opposite side of the world from the prime meridian. The International Date Line is one-half of one day or 12 time zones from the prime meridian. If you were traveling west across the International Date Line, you would lose one day. If you were traveling east across the International Date Line, you would gain one day.

Principles of contouring
A contour line is a line on a map representing an imaginary line on the ground that has the same elevation above sea level along its entire length. Contour intervals usually are given in even numbers or as a multiple of five. In mapping mountains, a large contour interval is used. Small contour intervals may be used where there are small differences in elevation.

Relief describes how much variation in elevation an area has. Rugged or high relief, describes an area of many hills and valleys. Gentle or low relief describes a plain area or a coastal region. Five general rules should be remembered in studying contour lines on a map.

1. Contour lines close around hills and basins or depressions. Hachure lines are used to show depressions. Hachures are short lines placed at right angles to the contour line and they always point toward the lower elevation.

2. Contour lines never cross. Contour lines are sometimes very close together. Each contour line represents a certain height above sea level.

3. Contour lines appear on both sides of an area where the slope reverses direction. Contour lines show where an imaginary horizontal plane would slice through a hillside or cut both sides of a valley.

4. Contour lines form V's that point upstream when they cross streams. Streams cut beneath the general elevation of the land surface, and contour lines follow a valley.

5. All contour lines either close (connect) or extend to the edge of the map. No map is large enough to have all its contour lines close.

Interpret maps and imagery

Like photographs, maps readily display information that would be impractical to express in words. Maps that show the shape of the land are called topographic maps. Topographic maps, which are also referred to as quadrangles, are generally classified according to publication scale. Relief refers to the difference in elevation between any two points. Maximum relief refers to the difference in elevation between the highest and lowest points in the area being considered. Relief determines the contour interval, which is the difference in elevation between succeeding contour lines that are used on topographic maps.

Map scales express the relationship between distance or area on the map to the true distance or area on the earth's surface. It is expressed as so many feet, (miles, meters, km, or degrees) per inch (cm), of the map.

Minerals

Minerals are natural inorganic compounds. They are solid with homogenous crystal structures. Crystal structures are the 3-D geometric arrangements of atoms within minerals. Though these mineral grains are often too small to see, they can be visualized by X-ray diffraction. Both chemical composition and crystal structure determine mineral type. The chemical composition of minerals can vary from purely elemental to simple salts to complex compounds. However, it is possible for two or more minerals to have identical chemical composition, but varied crystal structure. Such minerals are known as polymorphs. One example of polymorphs demonstrates how crystal structures influence the physical properties of minerals with the same chemical composition; diamonds and graphite. Both are made from carbon, but diamonds are extremely hard because the carbon atoms are arranged in a strong 3-D network while graphite is soft because the carbon atoms are present in sheets that slide past one another. There are over 4,400 minerals on Earth, which are organized into the following classes:

Silicate minerals are composed mostly of silicon and oxygen. This is the most abundant class of minerals on Earth and includes quartz, garnets, micas, and feldspars.

Carbonate class is composed of compounds including carbonate ions (including calcium carbonate, magnesium carbonate, and iron carbonate). They are common in marine environments, in caves (stalactites and stalagmites), and anywhere minerals can form via dissolution and precipitation. Nitrate and borate minerals are also in this class.

Sulfate minerals contain sulfate ions and are formed near bodies of water where slow evaporation allows precipitation of sulfates and halides. Sulfates include celestite, barite, and gypsum.

Halide minerals include all minerals formed from natural salts including calcium fluoride, sodium chloride, and ammonium chloride. Like the sulfides, these minerals are typically formed in evaporative settings. Minerals in this class include fluorite, halite, and sylvite.

Oxide class minerals contain oxide compounds including iron oxide, magnetite oxide, and chromium oxide. They are formed by various processes including precipitation and oxidation of other minerals. These minerals form many ores and are important in mining. Hematite, chromite, rutile, and magnetite are all examples of oxide minerals.

Sulfide minerals are formed from sulfide compounds such as iron sulfide, nickel iron sulfide and lead sulfide. Several important metal ores are members of this class. Minerals in this class include pyrite (fool's gold) and galena.

The phosphate class includes not only those containing phosphate ions, but any mineral with a tetrahedral molecular geometry in which an element is surrounded by four oxygen atoms. This can include elements such as phosphorous, arsenic, and antimony. Minerals in this class are important biologically, as they are common in teeth and bones. Phosphate, arsenate, vanadate, and antimonite minerals are all in this class.

Element class minerals are formed from pure elements, whether they are metallic, semi-metallic or non-metallic. Accordingly, minerals in this class include gold, silver, copper, bismuth, and graphite as well as natural alloys such as electrum and carbides.

Rocks

Rocks are simply aggregates of minerals. Rocks are classified by their differences in chemical composition and mode of formation. Generally, three classes are recognized; igneous, sedimentary, and metamorphic. However, it is common that one type of rock is transformed into another and this is known as the rock cycle.

Igneous rocks are formed from molten magma. There are two types of igeneous rock; volcanic and plutonic. As the name suggest, volcanic rock is formed when magma reaches the earth's surface as lava. Plutonic rock is also derived from magma, but it is formed when magma cools and crystallizes beneath surface of the Earth. Thus, both types of igneous rock are magma that has cooled either above (volcanic) or below (plutonic) the earth's crust. Examples of this type of rock include granite and obsidian glass.

Sedimentary rocks are formed by the layered deposition of inorganic and/or organic matter. Layers, or strata, of rock are laid down horizontally to form sedimentary rocks. Sedimentary rocks that form as mineral solutions (i.e., sea water) evaporate are called precipitate. Those that contain the remains of living organisms are termed biogenic. Finally, those that form from the freed fragments of other rocks are called clastic. Because the layers of sedimentary rocks reveal chronology and often contain fossils, these types of rock have been key in helping scientists understand the history of the earth. Chalk, limestone, sandstone, and shale are all examples of sedimentary rock.

Metamorphic rocks are created when rocks are subjected to high temperatures and pressures. The original rock, or protolith, may have been igneous, sedimentary or even an older metamorphic rock. The temperatures and pressures necessary to achieve transformation are higher than those observed on the Earth's surface and are high enough to alter the minerals in the protolith.

Because these rocks are formed within the Earth's crust, studying metamorphic rocks gives us clues to conditions in the Earth's mantle. In some metamorphic rocks, different colored bands are apparent. These result from strong pressures being applied from specific directions and is termed foliation. Examples of metamorphic rock include slate and marble.

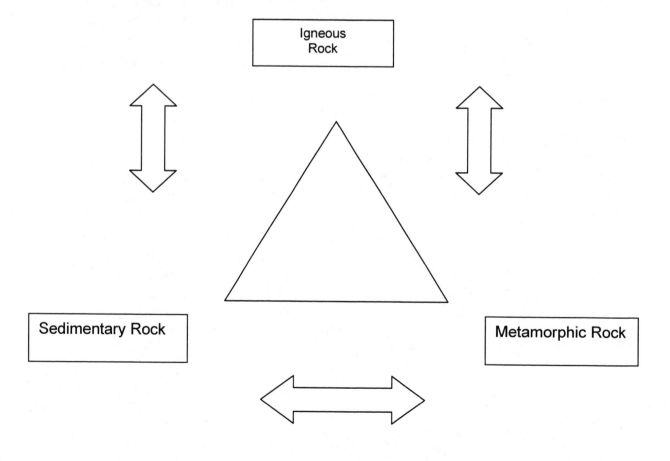

Soils

Soils are composed of particles of sand, clay, various minerals, tiny living organisms, and humus, plus the decayed remains of plants and animals. Soils are divided into three classes according to their texture. These classes are sandy soils, clay soils, and loamy soils.

Sandy soils are gritty, and their particles do not bind together firmly. Sandy soils are porous; water passes through them rapidly. Sandy soils do not hold much water.

Clay soils are smooth and greasy, their particles bind together firmly. Clay soils are moist and usually do not allow water to pass through easily.

Loamy soils feel somewhat like velvet and their particles clump together. Loamy soils are made up of sand, clay, and silt. Loamy soils hold water but some water can pass through.

In addition to three main classes, soils are further grouped into three major types based upon their composition. These groups are pedalfers, pedocals, and laterites.

Pedalfers form in the humid, temperate climate of the eastern United States. Pedalfer soils contain large amounts of iron oxide and aluminum-rich clays, making the soil a brown to reddish brown color. This soil supports forest type vegetation.

Pedocals are found in the western United States where the climate is dry and temperate. These soils are rich in calcium carbonate. This type of soil supports grasslands and brush vegetation.

Laterites are found where the climate is wet and tropical. Large amounts of water flows through this soil. Laterites are red-orange soils rich in iron and aluminum oxides. There is little humus and this soil is not very fertile.

Skill 5.2   Describe the characteristics and properties of the hydrosphere

Water Cycle

Water that falls to Earth in the form of rain and snow is called **precipitation.** Precipitation is part of a continuous process in which water at the Earth's surface evaporates, condenses into clouds, and returns to Earth. This process is termed the **water cycle**. The water located below the surface is called groundwater.

Water flow and collection

Water flows and is collected in a predictable manner. In most situations it runs across land and into small streams that feed larger bodies of water. All of the land that acts like a funnel for water flowing into a single larger body of water is known as a watershed or drainage basin. The watershed includes the streams and rivers that bear the water and the surfaces across which the water runs. Thus, the pollution load and general state of all the land within a watershed has an effect on the health and cleanliness of the body of water to which it drains. Large land features, such as mountains, separate watersheds from one another. However, some portion of water from one watershed may enter the groundwater and ultimately flow towards another adjacent watershed.

Not all water flows to the streams, rivers, and lakes that comprise the above ground water supply. Some water remains in the soil as ground water. Additionally, underground rivers are found in areas of karst topography, though these are relatively rare. It is more common for water to collect in underground aquifers. Aquifers are layers of permeable rock or loose material (gravel, sand, or silt) that hold water. Aquifers may be either confined or unconfined. Confined aquifers are deep in the ground and below the water table. Unconfined aquifers border on the water table. The water table is the level at which ground water exists and is always equal to atmospheric pressure. To visualize the entire ground water system, we can imagine a hole dug in wet sand at the beach and a small pool of water within the hole. The wet sand corresponds to the aquifer, the hole to a well or lake, and the level of water in the hole to the water table.

In some cases, people have created reservoirs, artificial storage areas that make large amounts of water readily available.   Reservoirs are most often created by damming rivers. A dam is built from cement, soil, or rock and the river fills the newly created reservoir. A reservoir may be created by building a dam either across a valley or around the entire perimeter of an artificial lake (a bunded dam). The former technique is more common and relies on natural features to form a watertight reservoir. However, such a feature must exist to allow this type of construction. A fully bunded dam does not require such a natural feature but does necessitate more construction since a waterproof structure must be built all the way around the reservoir. This structure is typically made from clay and/or cement. Since no river feeds such reservoirs, mechanical pumps are used to fill them from nearby water sources. Occasionally, watertight roofs are added to these reservoirs so they can be used to hold treated water. These are known as service reservoirs.

Skill 5.3   Analyze the earth's atmosphere, weather, and climate

Atmosphere

Dry air is composed of three basic components; dry gas, water vapor, and solid particles (dust from soil, etc.).

The most abundant dry gases in the atmosphere are:

(N_2)	Nitrogen	78.09 %	makes up about 4/5 of gases in atmosphere
(O_2)	Oxygen	20.95 %	
(Ar)	Argon	0.93 %	
(CO_2)	Carbon Dioxide	0.03 %	

The atmosphere is divided into four main layers based on temperature. These layers are labeled Troposphere, Stratosphere, Mesosphere, and Thermosphere.

Troposphere - this layer is the closest to the earth's surface and all weather phenomena occurs here as it is the layer with the most water vapor and dust. Air temperature decreases with increasing altitude. The average thickness of the troposphere is 7 miles (11 km).

Stratosphere - this layer contains very little water, clouds within this layer are extremely rare. The ozone layer is located in the upper portions of the stratosphere. Air temperature is fairly constant but does increase somewhat with height due to the absorption of solar energy and ultraviolet rays from the ozone layer.

Mesosphere - air temperature again decreases with height in this layer. It is the coldest layer with temperatures in the range of -100^0 C at the top.

Thermosphere - extends upward into space. Oxygen molecules in this layer absorb energy from the sun, causing temperatures to increase with height. The lower part of the thermosphere is called the ionosphere. Here charged particles or ions and free electrons can be found. When gases in the ionosphere are excited by solar radiation, the gases give off light and glow in the sky. These glowing lights are called the Aurora Borealis in the Northern Hemisphere and Aurora Australis in Southern Hemisphere. The upper portion of the thermosphere is called the exosphere. Gas molecules are very far apart in this layer. Layers of exosphere are also known as the Van Allen Belts and are held together by earth's magnetic field.

Movement of air

Energy is transferred in earth's atmosphere in three ways. Earth gets most of its energy from the sun in the form of waves. This transfer of energy by waves is termed **radiation**. The transfer of thermal energy through matter by actual contact of molecules is called **conduction**. For example, heated rocks and sandy beaches transfer heat to the surrounding air. The transfer of thermal energy due to air density differences is called **convection**. Convection currents circulate in a constant exchange of cold, dense air for less dense warm air.

Cloud formation and precipitation

Condensation or the removal of water above the earth's surface results in the formation of clouds. Generally, clouds develop in any air mass that becomes saturated or has a relative humidity of 100%. Certain processes that cool the temperature of an air mass to its dew point or frost point can cause saturation. There are four processes or any combination of these processes that create saturation and cause clouds to form:

1. Orographic uplift occurs when elevated land forces air to rise.
2. Convectional lifting is the result of surface heating of air at ground level. If enough heating occurs, the air rises, expands, and cools.
3. Convergence or frontal lifting occurs when two air masses come together. One of the air masses is usually warm and moist, while the other is cool and dry.
4. Radiative cooling usually occurs at night when the sun is no longer heating the ground and the surrounding air. The ground and the air begin to cool, forming fog.

Meteorology equipment

There are two kinds of weather instruments that measure air pressure; (1) the aneroid barometer and (2) the mercury barometer.

As air exerts varying pressures on a metal diaphragm within an **aneroid barometer**, a sensitive metal pointer linked to the diaphragm moves either up or down a graduated scale that indicates units of pressure.

A **mercury barometer** operates when atmospheric pressure pushes on a pool of mercury in an open dish in the center of which is placed an evacuated glass tube. Air pressure forces the pool of mercury up into the tube. The higher the air pressure; the higher up the tube the mercury rises. The tube is scaled to reflect units of atmospheric pressure in inches of Hg.

There are two kinds of weather instruments that measure relative humidity; (1) a psychrometer and (2), a hair gygrometer.

The **psychrometer** or "sling psychrometer", which is the preferred term used by meteorologists, consists of two identical mercury thermometers. In order to calculate the water vapor/moisture in the present air, one end of one thermometer is covered with a wick or clothlike cover which is dipped in water. Spinning the entire instrument allows evaporation of water from the wick. Measuring the difference between the two thermometer readings determines the relative humidity.

The hair hygrometer is another type of sensing method that indicates the contraction or expansion when recording relative humidity. The operating principle of a hair hygrometer relies on the fact the human hair stretches whenever it gets damp.

An **anemometer** measures wind speed and a **wind vane** measures wind direction.

Evangelista Torricelli (1608-1647), an Italian mathematician, developed the first barometer.

Galileo Galilei (1564-1642), an Italian astronomer and physicist invented the first thermometer.

Christoph Buys-Ballot (1817-1890), a former director of the Netherlands Meteorological Institute devised the "baric wind law". This is better known as the Buys-Ballot's Law. This law states that in the northern hemisphere, when a person stands with his back to the wind, the lowest pressure is always toward the left. In the southern hemisphere just the opposite occurs.

Analyze and predict weather

Every day every one of us is affected by weather. It may be in the form of a typical thunderstorm, bringing moist air and cumulonimbus clouds, or a severe storm with pounding winds that can cause either hurricanes or tornados (twisters). These are common terms, as well as blizzards or ice storms, that we can all identify with.

The daily newscast relates terms such as dew point and relative humidity and barometric pressure. Suddenly, all too common terms become clouded with terms more frequently used by a meteorologist (someone who forecasts weather). Dew point is the air temperature at which water vapor begins to condense. Relative humidity is the actual amount of water vapor in a certain volume of air compared to the maximum amount of water vapor that this air could hold at a given temperature.

Weather instruments that forecast weather include the aneroid barometer and the mercury barometer that measure air pressure. The air exerts varying pressures on a metal diaphragm that will then read air pressure. The mercury barometer operates when atmospheric pressure pushes on a pool of (mercury) in a glass tube. The higher the pressure, the higher up the tube mercury will rise.

Relative humidity is measured by two kinds of weather instruments, the psychrometer and the hair gygrometer. Relative humidity simply indicates the amount of moisture in the air. Relative humidity is defined as a ratio of existing amounts of water vapor and moisture in the air when compared to the maximum amount of moisture that the air can hold at the same given pressure and temperature. Relative humidity is stated as a percentage, so for example the relative humidity can be 100%.

If you were to analyze relative humidity from data, an example might be: If a parcel of air is saturated (meaning it now holds all the moisture it can hold at a given temperature), then the relative humidity is 100%.

Lesson Plans for teachers to analyze data and predict weather can be found at:

http://www.srh.weather.gov/srh/jetstream/synoptic/ll_analyze.htm

Analyzing Weather Maps
Once you can read a station plot you can begin to perform map analyses. Meteorologists use the station plots to draw lines of constant pressure (isobars), temperature (isotherms), and dewpoint (isodrosotherms) to achieve an understanding of the current state of the atmosphere. This knowledge ultimately leads to better weather forecasts and warnings.

Decoding these plots is easier than it may seem. The values are located in a form similar to a tic-tac-toe pattern.

In the upper left, the temperature is plotted in Fahrenheit. In this example, the temperature is 77°F.

Along the center, the cloud types are indicated. The top symbol is the high-level cloud type followed by the mid-level cloud type. The lowest symbol represents low-level cloud over a number which tells the height of the base of that cloud (in hundreds of feet). In this example, the high level cloud is cirrus, the mid-level cloud is Altocumulus and the low-level cloud is a cumulonimbus with a base height of 2000 feet.

At the upper right is the atmospheric pressure reduced to mean sea level in millibars (mb) to the nearest tenth with the leading 9 or 10 omitted. In this case the pressure would be 999.8 mb. If the pressure was plotted as 024 it would be 1002.4 mb. When trying to determine whether to add a 9 or 10 use the number that will give you a value closest to 1000 mb.

On the second row, the far left number is the visibility in miles. In this example, the visibility is 5 miles.

Next to the visibility is the present weather symbol. There 95 symbols which represent the weather that is either presently occurring or has ended within the previous hour. In this example, a light rain shower was occurring at the time of the observation.

The circle symbol in the center represents the amount of total cloud cover reported in eighths. This cloud cover includes all low, middle, and high level clouds. In this example, 7/8th of the sky was covered with clouds.

This number and symbol tell how much the pressure has changed (in tenths of millibars) in the past three hours and the trend in the change of the pressure during that same period. In this example, the pressure was steady, then fell (lowered) becoming 0.3 millibars LOWER than it was three hours ago.

These lines indicate wind direction and speed rounded to the nearest 5 knots. The longest line, extending from the sky cover plot, points in the direction that the wind is blowing **from**. Thus, in this case, the wind is blowing **from** the southwest. The shorter lines, called barbs, indicate the wind speed in knots (kt). The speed of the wind is calculated by the barbs. Each long barb represents 10 kt with short barbs representing 5 kt. In this example, the station plot contains two long barbs so the wind speed is 20 kt, or about 24 mph.

The 71 at the lower left is the dewpoint temperature. The dewpoint temperature is the temperature the air would have to cool to become saturated, or in other words reach a relative humidity of 100%.

The lower right area is reserved for the past weather, which is the most significant weather that has occurred within the past six hours excluding the most recent hour.

Skill 5.4 **Analyze the components of the solar system and universe and their interactions**

Two main hypotheses of the origin of the solar system are: (1) **the tidal hypothesis** and (2) **the condensation hypothesis**.

The tidal hypothesis proposes that the solar system began with a near collision of the sun and a large star. Some astronomers believe that as these two stars passed each other, the great gravitational pull of the large star extracted hot gases out of the sun. The mass from the hot gases started to orbit the sun, which then began to cool condensing into the nine planets (few astronomers support this theory).

The condensation hypothesis proposes that the solar system began with rotating clouds of dust and gas. Condensation occurred in the center forming the sun and smaller parts of the cloud formed the nine planets (this example is widely accepted).

The dominant scientific theory about the origin of the Universe, and consequently the Earth, is the **Big Bang Theory**. According to this theory, a point source exploded about 10 to 20 billion years ago throwing matter in all directions. Although this theory has never been proven, and probably never will be, it is supported by the fact that distant galaxies in every direction are moving away from us at great speeds.

Earth, itself, is believed to have been created 4.5 billion years ago as a solidified cloud of gases and dust left over from the creation of the sun. As millions of years passed, radioactive decay released energy that melted some of Earth's components. Over time, the heavier components sank to the center of the Earth and accumulated into the core. As the Earth cooled, a crust formed with natural depressions. Water rising from the interior of the Earth filled these depressions and formed the oceans. Slowly, the Earth acquired the appearance it has today.

Planets

There are nine planets in our solar system. They are: Mercury, Venus, Earth, Mars, Jupiter, Saturn, Uranus, Neptune, and Pluto. These nine planets are divided into two groups based on their distance from the sun. The groups are called inner and outer planets. The inner planets include: Mercury, Venus, Earth, and Mars. The outer planets include: Jupiter, Saturn, Uranus, Neptune and Pluto. In 2006, Pluto was reclassified as a minor planet.

Mercury -the closest planet to the sun. Its surface has craters and rocks. The atmosphere is composed of hydrogen, helium and sodium. Mercury was named after the Roman messenger god.

Venus -has a slow rotation when compared to earth. Venus and Uranus rotate in opposite directions from the other planets. This opposite rotation is called retrograde rotation. The surface of Venus is not visible due to the extensive cloud cover. The atmosphere is composed mostly of carbon dioxide. Sulfuric acid droplet in the dense cloud cover gives Venus a yellow appearance. Venus has a greater greenhouse effect than that observed on earth. The dense clouds of carbon dioxide trap heat. Venus was named after the Roman goddess of love.

Earth -considered a water planet with seventy percent of its surface covered with water. Gravity holds the masses of water in place. The different temperatures observed on earth allows for the different states of water to exist; solid, liquid or gas. The atmosphere is composed mainly of oxygen and nitrogen. Earth is the only planet that is known to support life.

Mars -the surface of Mars contains numerous craters, active and extinct volcanoes, ridges and valleys with extremely deep fractures. Iron oxide found in the dusty soil makes the surface seem rust colored and the skies seem pink in color. The atmosphere is composed of carbon dioxide, nitrogen, argon, oxygen and water vapor. Mars has polar regions with ice caps composed of water. Mars has two satellites. Mars was named after the Roman war god.

Jupiter -- largest planet in the solar system. Jupiter has 16 moons. The atmosphere is composed of hydrogen, helium, methane and ammonia. There are white colored bands of clouds indicating rising gas and dark colored bands of clouds indicating descending gases. This circulation is caused by the heat developed from the energy of Jupiter's core. Jupiter has a Great Red Spot that is thought to be a hurricane type cloud. Jupiter has a strong magnetic field.

Saturn -the second largest planet in the solar system. Saturn has beautiful rings of ice and rock and dust particles circling this planet. Saturn's atmosphere is composed of hydrogen, helium, methane and ammonia. Saturn has 20 plus satellites. Saturn was named after the Roman god of agriculture.

Uranus -the second largest planet in the solar system with retrograde revolution (Venus is the other retrograde planet). Uranus a gaseous planet, it has 10 dark rings and 15 satellites. Its atmosphere is composed of hydrogen, helium and methane. Uranus was named after the Greek god of the heavens.

Neptune -another gaseous planet with an atmosphere consisting of hydrogen, helium and methane. Neptune has 3 rings and 2 satellites. Neptune was named after the Roman sea god because its atmosphere (methane) has the same color as the sea.

Pluto -the smallest planet in the solar system. Pluto's atmosphere probably contains methane, ammonia and frozen water. Pluto has 1 satellite. Pluto revolves around the sun every 250 years. Pluto was named after the Roman god of the underworld. As of the summer of 2006, Pluto's status as a planet was controversial and it has since been reclassified.

Astronomers believe that **asteroids** are rocky fragments that may have been the remains of the birth of the solar system that never formed into a planet. Asteroids are found in the region between Mars and Jupiter.

Comets are masses of frozen gases, cosmic dust, and small rocky particles. Astronomers think that most comets originate in a dense comet cloud beyond Pluto. Comet consists of a nucleus, a coma, and a tail. A comet's tail always points away from the sun.

The most famous comet, **Halley's Comet**, is named after the person who first discovered it. It returns to the skies near earth every 75 to 76 years.

Meteoroids are composed of particles of rock and metal of various sizes. When a meteoroid travels through the earth's atmosphere friction causes its surface to heat up and it begins to burn. The burning meteoroid falling through the earth's atmosphere is now called a **meteor** or a "shooting star." **Meteorites** are meteors that strike the earth's surface. A physical example of the impact of a meteorite on the earth's surface can be seen in Arizona. The Barringer Crater is a huge meteor crater. There are many other such meteor craters found throughout the world.

Stars

A star is a ball of hot, glowing gas that is hot enough and dense enough to trigger nuclear reactions, which fuel the star. In comparing the mass, light production, and size of the sun to other stars, astronomers find that the Sun is a perfectly ordinary star. It behaves exactly the way they would expect a star of its size to behave. The main difference between the sun and other stars is that the sun is much closer to earth.

Most stars have masses similar to that of the sun. The majority of stars' masses are between 0.3 to 3.0 times the mass of the sun. Theoretical calculations indicate that in order to trigger nuclear reactions and to create its own energy— that is, to become a star—a body must have a mass greater than 7 percent of the mass of the sun. Astronomical bodies that are less massive than this become planets or objects called brown dwarfs. The largest accurately determined stellar mass is of a star called V382 Cygni and is 27 times that of the sun.

The range of brightness among stars is much larger than the range of mass. Astronomers measure the brightness of a star by measuring its magnitude and luminosity. Magnitude allows astronomers to rank how bright, comparatively, different stars appear to humans. Because of the way our eyes detect light, a lamp ten times more luminous than a second lamp will appear less than ten times brighter to human eyes. This discrepancy affects the magnitude scale, as does the tradition of giving brighter stars lower magnitudes. The lower a star's magnitude, the brighter it is. Stars with negative magnitudes are the brightest of all.

Magnitude is given in terms of absolute and apparent values. Absolute magnitude is a measurement of how bright a star would appear if viewed from a set distance away. Astronomers also measure a star's brightness in terms of its luminosity. A star's absolute luminosity or intrinsic brightness is the total amount of energy radiated by the star per second. Luminosity is often expressed in units of watts.

Results of Earth's motions and orientation

Earth is the third planet away from the sun in our solar system. Earth's numerous types of motion and states of orientation greatly effect global conditions, such as seasons, tides and lunar phases. The earth orbits the sun with a period of 365 days. During this orbit, the average distance between the earth and sun is 93 million miles. The shape of the earth's orbit around the sun deviates from the shape of a circle only slightly. This deviation, known as the earth's eccentricity, has a very small affect on the earth's climate. The earth is closest to the sun at perihelion, occurring around January 2nd of each year, and farthest from the sun at aphelion, occurring around July 2nd. Because the earth is closest to the sun in January, the northern winter is slightly warmer than the southern winter.

Seasons

The rotation axis of the earth is not perpendicular to the orbital (ecliptic) plane. The axis of the earth is tilted 23.45° from the perpendicular. The tilt of the earth's axis is known as the obliquity of the ecliptic, and is mainly responsible for the four seasons of the year by influencing the intensity of solar rays received by the northern and southern hemispheres. The four seasons, spring, summer, fall and winter, are extended periods of characteristic average temperature, rainfall, storm frequency and vegetation growth or dormancy. The effect of the earth's tilt on climate is best demonstrated at the solstices, the two days of the year when the sun is farthest from the earth's equatorial plane. At the Summer Solstice (June Solstice), the earth's tilt on its axis causes the northern hemisphere to the lean toward the sun, while the southern hemisphere leans away. Consequently, the northern hemisphere receives more intense rays from the Sun and experiences summer during this time, while the southern hemisphere experiences winter. At the Winter Solstice (December Solstice), it is the southern hemisphere that leans toward the sun and thus experiences summer. Spring and fall are produced by varying degrees of the same leaning toward or away from the Sun.

Tides

The orientation of and gravitational interaction between the earth and the moon are responsible for the ocean tides that occur on earth. The term "tide" refers to the cyclic rise and fall of large bodies of water. Gravitational attraction is defined as the force of attraction between all bodies in the universe. At the location on earth closest to the moon, the gravitational attraction of the moon draws seawater toward the moon in the form of a tidal bulge. On the opposite side of the earth, another tidal bulge forms in the direction away from the moon because at this point, the moon's gravitational pull is the weakest. "Spring tides" are especially strong tides that occur when the earth, sun and moon are in line, allowing both the sun and the moon to exert gravitational force on the earth and increase tidal bulge height. These tides occur during the full moon and the new moon. "Neap tides" are especially weak tides occurring when the gravitational forces of the moon and the sun are perpendicular to one another. These tides occur during quarter moons.

Lunar Phases

The earth's orientation in respect to the solar system is also responsible for our perception of the phases of the moon. As the earth orbits the sun with a period of 365 days, the moon orbits the earth every 27 days. As the moon circles the earth, its shape in the night sky appears to change. The changes in the appearance of the moon from earth are known as "lunar phases." These phases vary cyclically according to the relative positions of the moon, the earth and the sun. At all times, half of the moon is facing the sun and is thus illuminated by reflecting the sun's light. As the moon orbits the earth and the earth orbits the sun, the half of the moon that faces the sun changes. However, the moon is in synchronous rotation around the earth, meaning that nearly the same side of the moon faces the earth at all times. This side is referred to as the near side of the moon. Lunar phases occur as the earth and moon orbit the sun and the fractional illumination of the moon's near side changes.

When the sun and moon are on opposite sides of the earth, observers on earth perceive a "full moon," meaning the moon appears circular because the entire illuminated half of the moon is visible. As the moon orbits the earth, the moon "wanes" as the amount of the illuminated half of the moon that is visible from earth decreases. A gibbous moon is between a full moon and a half moon, or between a half moon and a full moon. When the sun and the moon are on the same side of earth, the illuminated half of the moon is facing away from earth, and the moon appears invisible. This lunar phase is known as the "new moon." The time between each full moon is approximately 29.53 days.

A list of all lunar phases includes:

- New Moon: the moon is invisible or the first signs of a crescent appear
- Waxing Crescent: the right crescent of the moon is visible
- First Quarter: the right quarter of the moon is visible
- Waxing Gibbous: only the left crescent is not illuminated
- Full Moon: the entire illuminated half of the moon is visible
- Waning Gibbous: only the right crescent of the moon is not illuminated
- Last Quarter: the left quarter of the moon is illuminated
- Waning Crescent: only the left crescent of the moon is illuminated

Viewing the moon from the southern hemisphere would cause these phases to occur in the opposite order.

Sample Test

Directions: Read each item and select the correct response. The answer key follows.

1. After an experiment, the scientist states that s/he believes a change in the color of a liquid is due to a change of pH. This is an example of _____ .

A. observing.

B. inferring.

C. measuring.

D. classifying.

2. When is a hypothesis formed?

A. Before the data is taken.

B. After the data is taken.

C. After the data is analyzed.

D. Concurrent with graphing the data.

3. Who determines the laws regarding the use of safety glasses in the classroom?

A. The state.

B. The school site.

C. The Federal government.

D. The district level.

4. If one inch equals 2.54 cm how many mm in 1.5 feet? (APPROXIMATELY)

A. 18 mm.

B. 1800 mm.

C. 460 mm.

D. 4,600 mm.

5. Which of the following instruments measures wind speed?

A. A barometer.

B. An anemometer.

C. A thermometer

D. A weather vane.

6. Sonar works by _____ .

A. timing how long it takes sound to reach a certain speed.

B. bouncing sound waves between two metal plates.

C. bouncing sound waves off an underwater object and timing how long it takes for the sound to return.

D. evaluating the motion and amplitude of sound.

7. The measure of the pull of the earth's gravity on an object is called _____ .

A. mass number.

B. atomic number.

C. mass.

D. weight.

8. Which reaction below is a decomposition reaction?

A. $HCl + NaOH \rightarrow NaCl + H_2O$

B. $C + O_2 \rightarrow CO_2$

C. $2H_2O \rightarrow 2H_2 + O_2$

D. $CuSO_4 + Fe \rightarrow FeSO_4 + Cu$

9. The Law of Conservation of Energy states that _____.

A. There must be the same number of products and reactants in any chemical equation.

B. Objects always fall toward large masses such as planets.

C. Energy is neither created nor destroyed, but may change form.

D. Lights must be turned off when not in use, by state regulation.

10. Which parts of an atom are located inside the nucleus?

A. electrons and neutrons.

B. protons and neutrons.

C. protons only.

D. neutrons only.

11. The elements in the modern Periodic Table are arranged _____ .

A. in numerical order by atomic number.

B. randomly.

C. in alphabetical order by chemical symbol.

D. in numerical order by atomic mass.

12. Carbon bonds with hydrogen by _____ .

A. ionic bonding.

B. non-polar covalent bonding.

C. polar covalent bonding.

D. strong nuclear force.

13. Vinegar is an example of a _____ .

A. strong acid.

B. strong base.

C. weak acid.

D. weak base.

14. Which of the following is not a nucleotide?

A. adenine.

B. alanine.

C. cytosine.

D. guanine.

15. When measuring the volume of water in a graduated cylinder, where does one read the measurement?

A. At the highest point of the liquid.

B. At the bottom of the meniscus curve.

C. At the closest mark to the top of the liquid.

D. At the top of the plastic safety ring.

16. A duck's webbed feet are examples of_____ .

A. mimicry.

B. structural adaptation.

C. protective resemblance.

D. protective coloration.

17. What cell organelle contains the cell's stored food?

A. Vacuoles.

B. Golgi Apparatus.

C. Ribosomes.

D. Lysosomes.

18. The first stage of mitosis is called _____ .

A. telophase.

B. anaphase.

C. prophase.

D. mitophase.

19. The Doppler Effect is associated most closely with which property of waves?

A. amplitude.

B. wavelength.

C. frequency.

D. intensity.

20. Viruses are responsible for many human diseases including all of the following *except* _____ ?

A. influenza.

B. A.I.D.S.

C. the common cold.

D. strep throat.

21. A series of experiments on pea plants formed by _____ showed that two invisible markers existed for each trait, and one marker dominated the other.

A. Pasteur.

B. Watson and Crick.

C. Mendel.

D. Mendeleev.

22. Formaldehyde should not be used in school laboratories for the following reason:

A. it smells unpleasant.

B. it is a known carcinogen.

C. it is expensive to obtain.

D. it is explosive.

23. Amino acids are carried to the ribosome in protein synthesis   by _____ .

A. transfer RNA (tRNA).

B. messenger RNA (mRNA).

C. ribosomal RNA (rRNA).

D. transformation RNA (trRNA).

24. When designing a scientific experiment, a student considers all the factors that may influence the results. The   process goal is to _____.

A. recognize and manipulate independent variables.

B. recognize and record independent variables.

C. recognize and manipulate dependent variables.

D. recognize and record dependent variables.

25. Since ancient times, people have been entranced with bird flight. What is the key to bird flight?

A. Bird wings are a particular shape and composition.

B. Birds flap their wings quickly enough to propel themselves.

C. Birds take advantage of tailwinds.

D. Birds take advantage of crosswinds.

26. Laboratory researchers have classified fungi as distinct from plants because the cell walls of fungi _____ .

A. contain chitin.

B. contain yeast.

C. are more solid.

D. are less solid.

27. In a fission reactor, "heavy water" is used to _____ .

A. terminate fission reactions.

B. slow down neutrons and moderate reactions.

C. rehydrate the chemicals.

D. initiate a chain reaction.

28. The transfer of heat by electromagnetic waves is called _____ .

A. conduction.

B. convection.

C. phase change.

D. radiation.

29. When heat is added to most solids, they expand. Why is this the case?

A. The molecules get bigger.

B. The faster molecular motion leads to greater distance between the molecules.

C. The molecules develop greater repelling electric forces.

D. The molecules form a more rigid structure.

30. The force of gravity on earth causes all bodies in free fall to _____ .

A. fall at the same speed.

B. accelerate at the same rate.

C. reach the same terminal velocity.

D. move in the same direction.

31. Sound waves are produced by _____ .

A. pitch.

B. noise.

C. vibrations.

D. sonar.

32. Resistance is measured in units called _____ .

A. watts.

B. volts.

C. ohms.

D. current.

33. Sound can be transmitted in all of the following *except* _____ .

A. air.

B. water.

C. a diamond.

D. a vacuum.

34. As a train approaches, the whistle sounds _____ .

A. higher, because it has a higher apparent frequency.

B. lower, because it has a lower apparent frequency.

C. higher, because it has a lower apparent frequency.

D. lower, because it has a higher apparent frequency.

35. The speed of light is different in different materials. This is responsible for _____ .

A. interference.

B. refraction.

C. reflection.

D. relativity.

36. A converging lens produces a real image _____ .

A. always.

B. never.

C. when the object is within one focal length of the lens.

D. when the object is further than one focal length from the lens.

37. The electromagnetic radiation with the longest wave length is/are _____ .

A. radio waves.

B. red light.

C. X-rays.

D. ultraviolet light.

38. Under a 440 power microscope, an object with diameter 0.1 millimeter   appears to have a diameter of _____ .

A. 4.4 millimeters.

B. 44 millimeters.

C. 440 millimeters.

D. 4400 millimeters.

39. Separating blood into blood cells and plasma involves the process of _____ .

A. electrophoresis.

B. spectrophotometry.

C. centrifugation.

D. chromatography.

40. Experiments may be done with any of the following animals except _____ .

A. birds.

B. invertebrates.

C. lower order life.

D. frogs.

41. For her first project of the year, a student is designing a science experiment to test the effects of light and water on plant growth. You should recommend that she _____.

A. manipulate the temperature also.

B. manipulate the water pH also.

C. determine the relationship between light and water unrelated to plant growth.

D. omit either water or light as a variable.

42. In a laboratory report, what is the abstract?

A. The abstract is a summary of the report, and is the first section of the report.

B. The abstract is a summary of the report, and is the last section of the report.

C. The abstract is predictions for future experiments, and is the first section of the report.

D. The abstract is predictions for future experiments, and is the last section of the report.

43. What is the scientific method?

A. It is the process of doing an experiment and writing a laboratory report.

B. It is the process of using open inquiry and repeatable results to establish theories.

C. It is the process of reinforcing scientific principles by confirming results.

D. It is the process of recording data and observations.

44. Identify the control in the following experiment: A student had four corn plants and was measuring photosynthetic rate (by measuring growth mass). Half of the plants were exposed to full (constant) sunlight, and the other half were kept in 50% (constant) sunlight.

A. The control is a set of plants grown in full (constant) sunlight.

B. The control is a set of plants grown in 50% (constant) sunlight.

C. The control is a set of plants grown in the dark.

D. The control is a set of plants grown in a mixture of natural levels of sunlight.

45. In an experiment measuring the growth of bacteria at different temperatures, what is the independent variable?

A. Number of bacteria.

B. Growth rate of bacteria.

C. Temperature.

D. Light intensity.

46. A scientific law_____.

A. proves scientific accuracy.

B. may never be broken.

C. may be revised in light of new data.

D. is the result of one excellent experiment.

47. Which is the correct order of methodology?

1. collecting data
2. planning a controlled experiment
3. drawing a conclusion
4. hypothesizing a result
5. re-visiting a hypothesis to answer a question

A. 1,2,3,4,5

B. 4,2,1,3,5

C. 4,5,1,3,2

D. 1,3,4,5,2

48. Which is the most desirable tool to use to heat substances in a middle school laboratory?

A. Alcohol burner.

B. Freestanding gas burner.

C. Bunsen burner.

D. Hot plate.

49. Newton's Laws are taught in science classes because _____.

A. they are the correct analysis of inertia, gravity, and forces.

B. they are a close approximation to correct physics, for usual Earth conditions.

C. they accurately incorporate relativity into studies of forces.

D. Newton was a well-respected scientist in his time.

50. Which of the following is most accurate?

A. Mass is always constant; Weight may vary by location.

B. Mass and Weight are both always constant.

C. Weight is always constant; Mass may vary by location.

D. Mass and Weight may both vary by location.

51. Chemicals should be stored

A. in the principal's office.

B. in a dark room.

C. in an off-site research facility.

D. according to their reactivity with other substances.

52. Which of the following is the worst choice for a school laboratory activity?

A. A genetics experiment tracking the fur color of mice.

B. Dissection of a preserved fetal pig.

C. Measurement of goldfish respiration rate at different temperatures.

D. Pithing a frog to watch the circulatory system.

53. Who should be notified in the case of a serious chemical spill?

A. The custodian.

B. The fire department or their municipal authority.

C. The science department chair.

D. The School Board.

54. A scientist exposes mice to cigarette smoke, and notes that their lungs develop tumors. Mice that were not exposed to the smoke do not develop as many tumors. Which of the following conclusions may be drawn from these results?

I. Cigarette smoke causes lung tumors.

II. Cigarette smoke exposure has a positive correlation with lung tumors in mice.

III. Some mice are predisposed to develop lung tumors.

IV. Mice are often a good model for humans in scientific research.

A. I and II only.

B. II only.

C. I, II, and III only.

D. II and IV only.

55. In which situation would a science teacher be legally liable?

A. The teacher leaves the classroom for a telephone call and a student slips and injures him/herself.

B. A student removes his/her goggles and gets acid in his/her eye.

C. A faulty gas line in the classroom causes a fire.

D. A student cuts him/herself with a dissection scalpel.

56. Which of these is the best example of 'negligence'?

A. A teacher fails to give oral instructions to those with reading disabilities.

B. A teacher fails to exercise ordinary care to ensure safety in the classroom.

C. A teacher displays inability to supervise a large group of students.

D. A teacher reasonably anticipates that an event may occur, and plans accordingly.

57. Which item should always be used when handling glassware?

A. Tongs.

B. Safety goggles.

C. Gloves.

D. Buret stand.

58. Which of the following is *not* a necessary characteristic of living things?

A. Movement.

B. Reduction of local entropy.

C. Ability to cause change in local energy form.

D. Reproduction.

59. What are the most significant and prevalent elements in the biosphere?

A. Carbon, Hydrogen, Oxygen, Nitrogen, Phosphorus.

B. Carbon, Hydrogen, Sodium, Iron, Calcium.

C. Carbon, Oxygen, Sulfur, Manganese, Iron.

D. Carbon, Hydrogen, Oxygen, Nickel, Sodium, Nitrogen.

60. All of the following measure energy *except* for _____

A. joules.

B. calories.

C. watts.

D. ergs.

61. Identify the correct sequence of organization of living things from lower to higher order:

A. Cell, Organelle, Organ, Tissue, System, Organism.

B. Cell, Tissue, Organ, Organelle, System, Organism.

C. Organelle, Cell, Tissue, Organ, System, Organism.

D. Organelle, Tissue, Cell, Organ, System, Organism.

62. Which kingdom is comprised of organisms made of one cell with no nuclear membrane?

A. Monera.

B. Protista.

C. Fungi.

D. Algae.

63. Which of the following is found in the least abundance in organic molecules?

A. Phosphorus.

B. Potassium.

C. Carbon.

D. Oxygen.

64. Catalysts assist reactions by _____ .

A. lowering effective activation energy.

B. maintaining precise pH levels.

C. keeping systems at equilibrium.

D. adjusting reaction speed.

65. Accepted procedures for preparing solutions should be made with _____ .

A. alcohol.

B. hydrochloric acid.

C. distilled water.

D. tap water.

66. Enzymes speed up reactions by _____ .

A. utilizing ATP.

B. lowering pH, allowing reaction speed to increase.

C. increasing volume of substrate.

D. lowering energy of activation.

67. When you step out of the shower, the floor feels colder on your feet than the bathmat. Which of the following is the correct explanation for this phenomenon?

A. The floor is colder than the bathmat.

B. Your feet have a chemical reaction with the floor, but not the bathmat.

C. Heat is conducted more easily into the floor.

D. Water is absorbed from your feet into the bathmat.

68. Which of the following is *not* considered ethical behavior for a scientist?

A. Using unpublished data and citing the source.

B. Publishing data before other scientists have had a chance to replicate results.

C. Collaborating with other scientists from different laboratories.

D. Publishing work with an incomplete list of citations.

69. The chemical equation for water formation is: $2H_2 + O_2 \rightarrow 2H_2O$. Which of the following is an *incorrect* interpretation of this equation?

A. Two moles of hydrogen gas and one mole of oxygen gas combine to make two moles of water.

B. Two grams of hydrogen gas and one gram of oxygen gas combine to make two grams of water.

C. Two molecules of hydrogen gas and one molecule of oxygen gas combine to make two molecules of water.

D. Four atoms of hydrogen (combined as a diatomic gas) and two atoms ofoxygen (combined as a diatomic gas) combine to make two molecules of water.

70. Energy is measured with the same units as _____.

A. force.

B. momentum.

C. work.

D. power.

71. If the volume of a confined gas is increased, what happens to the pressure of the gas? You may assume that the gas behaves ideally, and that temperature and number of gas molecules remain constant.

A. The pressure increases.

B. The pressure decreases.

C. The pressure stays the same.

D. There is not enough information given to answer this question.

72. A product of anaerobic respiration in animals is _____.

A. carbon dioxide.

B. lactic acid.

C. oxygen.

D. sodium chloride

73. A Newton is fundamentally a measure of _____ .

force.

momentum.

energy.

gravity.

74. Which change does *not* affect enzyme rate?

A. Increase the temperature.

B. Add more substrate.

C. Adjust the pH.

D. Use a larger cell.

75. Which of the following types of rock are made from magma?

A. Fossils

B. Sedimentary

C. Metamorphic

D. Igneous

76. Which of the following is *not* an acceptable way for a student to acknowledge sources in a laboratory report?

A. The student tells his/her teacher what sources s/he used to write the report.

B. The student uses footnotes in the text, with sources cited, but not in correct MLA format.

C. The student uses endnotes in the text, with sources cited, in correct MLA format.

D. The student attaches a separate bibliography, noting each use of sources.

77. Animals with a notochord or backbone are in the phylum

A. Arthropoda.

B. Chordata.

C. Mollusca.

D. Mammalia.

78. Which of the following is a correct explanation for scientific 'evolution'?

A. Giraffes need to reach higher for leaves to eat, so their necks stretch. The giraffe babies are then born with longer necks. Eventually, there are more long-necked giraffes in the population.

B. Giraffes with longer necks are able to reach more leaves, so they eat more and have more babies than other giraffes. Eventually, there are more long-necked giraffes in the population.

C. Giraffes want to reach higher for leaves to eat, so they release enzymes into their bloodstream, which in turn causes fetal development of longer-necked giraffes. Eventually, there are more long-necked giraffes in the population.

D. Giraffes with long necks are more attractive to other giraffes, so they get the best mating partners and have more babies. Eventually, there are more long-necked giraffes in the population.

79. Which of the following is a correct definition for 'chemical equilibrium'?

A. Chemical equilibrium is when the forward and backward reaction rates are equal. The reaction may continue to proceed forward and backward.

B. Chemical equilibrium is when the forward and backward reaction rates are equal, and equal to zero. The reaction does not continue.

C. Chemical equilibrium is when there are equal quantities of reactants and products.

D. Chemical equilibrium is when acids and bases neutralize each other fully.

80. Which of the following data sets is properly represented by a bar graph?

A. Number of people choosing to buy cars, vs. Color of car bought.

B. Number of people choosing to buy cars, vs. Age of car customer.

C. Number of people choosing to buy cars, vs. Distance from car lot to customer home.

D. Number of people choosing to buy cars, vs. Time since last car purchase.

81. In a science experiment, a student needs to dispense very small measured amounts of liquid into a well-mixed solution. Which of the following is the best choice for his/her equipment to use?

A. Buret with Buret Stand, Stir-plate, Stirring Rod, Beaker.

B. Buret with Buret Stand, Stir-plate, Beaker.

C. Volumetric Flask, Dropper, Graduated Cylinder, Stirring Rod.

D. Beaker, Graduated Cylinder, Stir-plate.

82. A laboratory balance is most appropriately used to measure the mass of which of the following?

A. Seven paper clips.

B. Three oranges.

C. Two hundred cells.

D. One student's elbow.

83. All of the following are measured in units of length, *except* for:

A. Perimeter.

B. Distance.

C. Radius.

D. Area.

84. What is specific gravity?

A. The mass of an object.

B. The ratio of the density of a substance to the density of water.

C. Density.

D. The pull of the earth's gravity on an object.

85. What is the most accurate description of the Water Cycle?

A. Rain comes from clouds, filling the ocean. The water then evaporates and becomes clouds again.

B. Water circulates from rivers into groundwater and back, while water vapor circulates in the atmosphere.

C. Water is conserved except for chemical or nuclear reactions, and any drop of water could circulate through clouds, rain, ground-water, and surface-water.

D. Weather systems cause chemical reactions to break water into its atoms.

86. The scientific name *Canis familiaris* refers to the animal's

_____.

A. kingdom and phylum.

B. genus and species.

C. class and species.

D. type and family.

87. Members of the same animal species _____ .

A. look identical.

B. never adapt differently.

C. are able to reproduce with one another.

D. are found in the same location.

88. Which of the following is/are true about scientists?

I. Scientists usually work alone.
II. Scientists usually work with other scientists.
III. Scientists achieve more prestige from new discoveries than from replicating established results.
IV. Scientists keep records of their own work, but do not publish it for outside review.

I and IV only.

II only.

II and III only.

D. I and IV only.

89. What is necessary for ion diffusion to occur spontaneously?

A. Carrier proteins.

B. Energy from an outside source.

C. A concentration gradient.

D. Cell flagellae.

90. All of the following are considered Newton's Laws *except* for:

A. An object in motion will continue in motion unless acted upon by an outside force.

B. For every action force, there is an equal and opposite reaction force.

C. Nature abhors a vacuum.

D. Mass can be considered the ratio of force to acceleration.

91. A cup of hot liquid and a cup of cold liquid are both sitting in a room at comfortable room temperature and humidity. Both cups are thin plastic. Which of the following is a true statement?

A. There will be fog on the outside of the hot liquid cup, and also fog on the outside of the cold liquid cup.

B. There will be fog on the outside of the hot liquid cup, but not on the cold liquid cup.

C. There will be fog on the outside of the cold liquid cup, but not on the hot liquid cup.

D. There will not be fog on the outside of either cup.

92. A ball rolls down a smooth hill. You may ignore air resistance. Which of the following is a true statement?

A. The ball has more energy at the start of its descent than just before it hits the bottom of the hill, because it is higher up at the beginning.

B. The ball has less energy at the start of its descent than just before it hits the bottom of the hill, because it is moving more quickly at the end.

C. The ball has the same energy throughout its descent, because positional energy is converted to energy of motion.

D. The ball has the same energy throughout its descent, because a single object (such as a ball) cannot gain or lose energy.

93. A long silver bar has a temperature of 50 degrees Celsius at one end and 0 degrees Celsius at the other end. The bar will reach thermal equilibrium (barring outside influence) by the process of heat _____.

A. conduction.

B. convection.

C. radiation.

D. phase change.

94. _____ are cracks in the plates of the earth's crust, along which the plates move.

A. Faults.

B. Ridges.

C. Earthquakes.

D. Volcanoes.

95. Fossils are usually found in _____ rock.

A. igneous.

B. sedimentary.

C. metamorphic.

D. cumulus.

96. Which of the following is *not* a common type of acid in 'acid rain' or acidified surface water?

A. Nitric acid.

B. Sulfuric acid.

C. Carbonic acid.

D. Hydrofluoric acid.

97. Which of the following is *not* true about phase change in matter?

A. Solid water and liquid ice can coexist at water's freezing point.

B. At 7 degrees Celsius, water is always in liquid phase.

C. Matter changes phase when enough energy is gained or lost.

D. Different phases of matter are characterized by differences in molecular motion.

98. Which of the following is the longest (largest) unit of geological time?

A. Solar Year.

B. Epoch.

C. Period.

D. Era.

99. Extensive use of antibacterial soap has been found to increase the virulence of certain infections in hospitals. Which of the following might be an explanation for this phenomenon?

A. Antibacterial soaps do not kill viruses.

B. Antibacterial soaps do not incorporate the same antibiotics used as medicine.

C. Antibacterial soaps kill a lot of bacteria, and only the hardiest ones survive to reproduce.

D. Antibacterial soaps can be very drying to the skin.

100. Which of the following is a correct explanation for astronaut 'weightlessness'?

A. Astronauts continue to feel the pull of gravity in space, but they are so far from planets that the force is small.

B. Astronauts continue to feel the pull of gravity in space, but spacecraft have such powerful engines that those forces dominate, reducing effective weight.

C. Astronauts do not feel the pull of gravity in space, because space is a vacuum.

D. Astronauts do not feel the pull of gravity in space, because black hole forces dominate the force field, reducing their masses.

101. The theory of 'sea floor spreading' explains _____.

A. the shapes of the continents.

B. how continents collide.

C. how continents move apart.

D. how continents sink to become part of the ocean floor.

102. Which of the following animals are most likely to live in a tropical rain forest?

A. Reindeer.

B. Monkeys.

C. Puffins.

D. Bears.

103. Which of the following is *not* a type of volcano?

A. Shield Volcanoes.

B. Composite Volcanoes.

C. Stratus Volcanoes.

D. Cinder Cone Volcanoes.

104. Which of the following is *not* a property of metalloids?

A. Metalloids are solids at standard temperature and pressure.

B. Metalloids can conduct electricity to a limited extent.

C. Metalloids are found in groups 13 through 17.

D. Metalloids all favor ionic bonding.

105. Which of these is a true statement about loamy soil?

A. Loamy soil is gritty and porous.

B. Loamy soil is smooth and a good barrier to water.

C. Loamy soil is hostile to microorganisms.

D. Loamy soil is velvety and clumpy.

106. Lithification refers to the process by which unconsolidated sediments are transformed into

_____.

A. metamorphic rocks.

B. sedimentary rocks.

C. igneous rocks.

D. lithium oxide.

107. Igneous rocks can be classified according to which of the following?

A. Texture.

B. Composition.

C. Formation process.

D. All of the above.

108. Which of the following is the most accurate definition of a non-renewable resource?

A. A nonrenewable resource is never replaced once used.

B. A nonrenewable resource is replaced on a timescale that is very long relative to human life-spans.

C. A nonrenewable resource is a resource that can only be manufactured by humans.

D. A nonrenewable resource is a species that has already become extinct.

109. The theory of 'continental drift' is supported by which of the following?

A. The way the shapes of South America and Europe fit together.

B. The way the shapes of Europe and Asia fit together.

C. The way the shapes of South America and Africa fit together.

D. The way the shapes of North America and Antarctica fit together.

110. When water falls to a cave floor and evaporates, it may deposit calcium carbonate. This process leads to the formation of which of the following?

A. Stalactites.

B. Stalagmites.

C. Fault lines.

D. Sedimentary rocks.

111. A child has type O blood. Her father has type A blood, and her mother has type B blood. What are the genotypes of the father and mother, respectively?

A. AO and BO.

B. AA and AB.

C. OO and BO.

D. AO and BB.

112. Which of the following is the best definition for 'meteorite'?

A. A meteorite is a mineral composed of mica and feldspar.

B. A meteorite is material from outer space, that has struck the earth's surface.

C. A meteorite is an element that has properties of both metals and nonmetals.

D. A meteorite is a very small unit of length measurement.

113. A white flower is crossed with a red flower. Which of the following is a sign of incomplete dominance?

A. Pink flowers.

B. Red flowers.

C. White flowers.

D. No flowers.

114. What is the source for most of the United States' drinking water?

A. Desalinated ocean water.

B. Surface water (lakes, streams, mountain runoff).

C. Rainfall into municipal reservoirs.

D. Groundwater.

115. Which is the correct sequence of insect development?

A. Egg, pupa, larva, adult.

B. Egg, larva, pupa, adult.

C. Egg, adult, larva, pupa.

D. Pupa, egg, larva, adult.

116. A wrasse (fish) cleans the teeth of other fish by eating away plaque. This is an example of _____ between the fish.

A. parasitism.

B. symbiosis (mutualism).

C. competition.

D. predation.

117. What is the main obstacle to using nuclear fusion for obtaining electricity?

A. Nuclear fusion produces much more pollution than nuclear fission.

B. There is no obstacle; most power plants us nuclear fusion today.

C. Nuclear fusion requires very high temperature and activation energy.

D. The fuel for nuclear fusion is extremely expensive.

118. Which of the following is a true statement about radiation exposure and air travel?

A. Air travel exposes humans to radiation, but the level is not significant for most people.

B. Air travel exposes humans to so much radiation that it is recommended as a method of cancer treatment.

C. Air travel does not expose humans to radiation.

D. Air travel may or may not expose humans to radiation, but it has not yet been determined.

119. Which process(es) result(s) in a haploid chromosome number?

A. Mitosis.

B. Meiosis.

C. Both mitosis and meiosis.

D. Neither mitosis nor meiosis.

120. Which of the following is *not* a member of Kingdom Fungi?

A. Mold.

B. Blue-green algae.

C. Mildew.

D. Mushrooms.

121. Which of the following organisms use spores to reproduce?

A. Fish.

B. Flowering plants.

C. Conifers.

D. Ferns.

122. What is the main difference between the 'condensation hypothesis' and the 'tidal hypothesis' for the origin of the solar system?

A. The tidal hypothesis can be tested, but the condensation hypothesis cannot.

B. The tidal hypothesis proposes a near collision of two stars pulling on each other, but the condensation hypothesis proposes condensation of rotating clouds of dust and gas.

C. The tidal hypothesis explains how tides began on planets such as Earth, but the condensation hypothesis explains how water vapor became liquid on Earth.

D. The tidal hypothesis is based on Aristotelian physics, but the condensation hypothesis is based on Newtonian mechanics.

123. Which of the following units is *not* a measure of distance?

A. AU (astronomical unit).

B. Light year.

C. Parsec.

D. Lunar year.

124. The salinity of ocean water is closest to _____ .

A. 0.035 %

B. 0.35 %

C. 3.5 %

D. 35 %

125. Which of the following will not change in a chemical reaction?

A. Number of moles of products.

B. Atomic number of one of the reactants.

C. Mass (in grams) of one of the reactants.

D. Rate of reaction.

Answer Key

1. B	26. A	51. D	76. A	101. C
2. A	27. B	52. D	77. B	102. B
3. A	28. D	53. B	78. B	103. C
4. C	29. B	54. B	79. A	104. D
5. B	30. B	55. A	80. A	105. D
6. C	31. C	56. B	81. B	106. B
7. D	32. C	57. B	82. A	107. D
8. C	33. D	58. A	83. D	108. B
9. C	34. A	59. A	84. B	109. C
10. B	35. B	60. C	85. C	110. B
11. A	36. D	61. C	86. B	111. A
12. C	37. A	62. A	87. C	112. B
13. C	38. B	63. B	88. C	113. A
14. B	39. C	64. A	89. C	114. D
15. B	40. A	65. C	90. C	115. B
16. B	41. D	66. D	91. C	116. B
17. A	42. A	67. C	92. C	117. C
18. C	43. B	68. D	93. A	118. A
19. C	44. A	69. B	94. A	119. B
20. D	45. C	70. C	95. B	120. B
21. C	46. C	71. B	96. D	121. D
22. B	47. B	72. B	97. B	122. B
23. A	48. D	73. A	98. D	123. D
24. A	49. B	74. D	99. C	124. C
25. A	50. A	75. D	100. A	125. B

Sample Questions with Rationales

1. After an experiment, the scientist states that s/he believes a change in color is due to a change in pH. This is an example of

A. observing.

B. inferring.

C. measuring.

D. classifying.

B. Inferring.

To answer this question, note that the scientist has observed a change in color, and has then made a guess as to its reason. This is an example of inferring. The scientist has not measured or classified in this case. Although s/he has observed [the color change], the explanation of this observation is **inferring (B)**.

2. When is a hypothesis formed?

A. Before the data is taken.

B. After the data is taken.

C. After the data is analyzed.

D. While the data is being graphed.

A. Before the data is taken.

A hypothesis is an educated guess, made before undertaking an experiment. The hypothesis is then evaluated based on the observed data. Therefore, the hypothesis must be formed before the data is taken, not during or after the experiment. This is consistent only with **answer (A)**.

3. Who determines the laws regarding the use of safety glasses in the classroom?

A. The state government.

B. The school site.

C. The federal government.

D. The local district.

A. The state government.

Health and safety regulations are set by the state government, and apply to all school districts. Federal regulations may accompany specific federal grants, and local districts or school sites may enact local guidelines that are stricter than the state standards. All schools, however, must abide by safety precautions as set by state government. This is consistent only with **answer (A)**.

4. If one inch equals 2.54 centimeters, how many millimeters are in 1.5 feet? (Approximately)

A. 18

B. 1800

C. 460

D. 4600

C. 460

To solve this problem, note that if one inch is 2.54 centimeters, then 1.5 feet (which is 18 inches), must be (18)(2.54) centimeters, i.e. approximately 46 centimeters. Because there are ten millimeters in a centimeter, this is approximately 460 millimeters:

(1.5 ft) (12 in/ft) (2.54 cm/in) (10 mm/cm) = (1.5) (12) (2.54) (10) mm = 457.2 mm

This is consistent only with **answer (C)**.

5. Which of the following instruments measures wind speed?

A. Barometer.

B. Anemometer.

C. Thermometer.

D. Weather Vane.

B. Anemometer.

An anemometer is a device to measure wind speed, while a barometer measures pressure, a thermometer measures temperature, and a weather vane indicates wind direction. This is consistent only with **answer (B).**

If you chose "barometer," here is an old physics joke to console you:

A physics teacher asks a student the following question:
 "Suppose you want to find out the height of a building, and the only tool you have is a barometer. How could you find out the height?"
 (The teacher hopes that the student will remember that pressure is inversely proportional to height, and will measure the pressure at the top of the building and then use the data to calculate the height of the building.)
 "Well," says the student, "I could tie a string to the barometer and lower it from the top of the building, and then measure the amount of string required."
 "You could," answers the teacher, "but try to think of a method that uses your physics knowledge from our class."
 "All right," replies the student, "I could drop the barometer from the roof and measure the time it takes to fall, and then use free-fall equations to calculate the height from which it fell."
 "Yes," says the teacher, "but what about using the barometer per se?"
 "Oh," answers the student, "I could find the building superintendent, and offer to exchange the barometer for a set of blueprints, and look up the height!"

6. Sonar works by _____

A. timing how long it takes sound to reach a certain speed.

B. bouncing sound waves between two metal plates.

C. bouncing sound waves off an object and timing how long it takes for the sound to return.

D. evaluating the motion and amplitude of sound.

C. Bouncing sound waves off an object and timing how long it takes for the sound to return.

Sonar is used to measure distances. Sound waves are sent out, and the time is measured for the sound to hit an obstacle and bounce back. By using the known speed of sound, observers (or machines) can calculate the distance to the obstacle. This is consistent only with **answer (C).**

7. The measure of the pull of Earth's gravity on an object is called

A. mass number.

B. atomic number.

C. mass.

D. weight.

D. Weight.

To answer this question, recall that mass number is the total number of protons and neutrons in an atom, atomic number is the number of protons in an atom, and mass is the amount of matter in an object. The only remaining **choice is (D)**, weight, which is correct because weight is the force of gravity on an object.

8. Which reaction below is a decomposition reaction?

A. $HCl + NaOH \rightarrow NaCl + H_2O$

B. $C + O_2 \rightarrow CO_2$

C. $2H_2O \rightarrow 2H_2 + O_2$

D. $CuSO_4 + Fe \rightarrow FeSO_4 + Cu$

C. $2H_2O \rightarrow 2H_2 + O_2$

To answer this question, recall that a decomposition reaction is one in which there are fewer reactants (on the left) than products (on the right). This is consistent only with **answer (C).** Meanwhile, note that answer (A) shows a double-replacement reaction (in which two sets of ions switch bonds), answer (B) shows a synthesis reaction (in which there are fewer products than reactants), and answer (D) shows a single-replacement reaction (in which one substance replaces another in its bond, but the other does not get a new bond).

9. The Law of Conservation of Energy states that

A. there must be the same number of products and reactants in any chemical equation.

B. objects always fall toward large masses such as planets.

C. energy is neither created nor destroyed, but may change form.

D. lights must be turned off when not in use, by state regulation.

C. Energy is neither created nor destroyed, but may change form.

Answer (C) is a summary of the Law of Conservation of Energy (for non-nuclear reactions). In other words, energy can be transformed into various forms such as kinetic, potential, electric, or heat energy, but the total amount of energy remains constant. Answer (A) is untrue, as demonstrated by many synthesis and decomposition reactions. Answers (B) and (D) may be sensible, but they are not relevant in this case. Therefore, the **answer is (C).**

10. Which parts of an atom are located inside the nucleus?

A. Protons and Electrons.

B. Protons and Neutrons.

C. Protons only.

D. Neutrons only.

B. Protons and Neutrons.

Protons and neutrons are located in the nucleus, while electrons move around outside the nucleus. This is consistent only with **answer (B)**.

11. The elements in the modern Periodic Table are arranged

A. in numerical order by atomic number.

B. randomly.

C. in alphabetical order by chemical symbol.

D. in numerical order by atomic mass.

A. In numerical order by atomic number.

Although the first periodic tables were arranged by atomic mass, the modern table is arranged by atomic number, i.e. the number of protons in each element. (This allows the element list to be complete and unique.) The elements are not arranged either randomly or in alphabetical order. The answer to this question is **therefore (A)**.

12. Carbon bonds with hydrogen by

A. ionic bonding.

B. non-polar covalent bonding.

C. polar covalent bonding.

D. strong nuclear force.

C. Polar covalent bonding.

Each carbon atom contains four valence electrons, while each hydrogen atom contains one valence electron. A carbon atom can bond with one or more hydrogen atoms, such that two electrons are shared in each bond. This is covalent bonding, because the electrons are shared. (In ionic bonding, atoms must gain or lose electrons to form ions. The ions are then electrically attracted in oppositely-charged pairs.) Covalent bonds are always polar when between two non-identical atoms, so this bond must be polar. ("Polar" means that the electrons are shared unequally, forming a pair of partial charges, i.e. poles.) In any case, the strong nuclear force is not relevant to this problem. The answer to this question is **therefore (C)**.

13. Vinegar is an example of a _____

A. strong acid.

B. strong base.

C. weak acid.

D. weak base.

C. Weak acid.

The main ingredient in vinegar is acetic acid, a weak acid. Vinegar is a useful acid in science classes, because it makes a frothy reaction with bases such as baking soda (e.g. in the quintessential volcano model). Vinegar is not a strong acid, such as hydrochloric acid, because it does not dissociate as fully or cause as much corrosion. It is not a base. Therefore, the **answer is (C)**.

14. Which of the following is not a nucleotide?

A. Adenine.

B. Alanine.

C. Cytosine.

D. Guanine.

B. Alanine.

Alanine is an amino acid. Adenine, cytosine, guanine, thymine, and uracil are nucleotides. The correct **answer is (B).**

15. When measuring the volume of water in a graduated cylinder, where does one read the measurement?

A. At the highest point of the liquid.

B. At the bottom of the meniscus curve.

C. At the closest mark to the top of the liquid.

D. At the top of the plastic safety ring.

B. At the bottom of the meniscus curve.

To measure water in glass, you must look at the top surface at eye-level, and ascertain the location of the bottom of the meniscus (the curved surface at the top of the water). The meniscus forms because water molecules adhere to the sides of the glass, which is a slightly stronger force than their cohesion to each other. This leads to a U-shaped top of the liquid column, the bottom of which gives the most accurate volume measurement. (Other liquids have different forces, e.g. mercury in glass, which has a convex meniscus.) This is consistent only with **answer (B).**

16. A duck's webbed feet are examples of

A. mimicry.

B. structural adaptation.

C. protective resemblance.

D. protective coloration.

B. Structural adaptation.

Ducks (and other aquatic birds) have webbed feet, which makes them more efficient swimmers. This is most likely due to evolutionary patterns where webbed-footed-birds were more successful at feeding and reproducing, and eventually became the majority of aquatic birds. Because the structure of the duck adapted to its environment over generations, this is termed 'structural adaptation'. Mimicry, protective resemblance, and protective coloration refer to other evolutionary mechanisms for survival. The answer to this question is **therefore (B)**.

17. What cell organelle contains the cell's stored food?

A. Vacuoles.

B. Golgi Apparatus.

C. Ribosomes.

D. Lysosomes.

A. Vacuoles.

In a cell, the sub-parts are called organelles. Of these, the vacuoles hold stored food (and water and pigments). The Golgi Apparatus sorts molecules from other parts of the cell; the ribosomes are sites of protein synthesis; the lysosomes contain digestive enzymes. This is consistent only with **answer (A)**.

18. The first stage of mitosis is called _____

A. telophase.

B. anaphase.

C. prophase.

D. mitophase.

C. Prophase.

In mitosis, the division of somatic cells, prophase is the stage where the cell enters mitosis. The four stages of mitosis, in order, are: prophase, metaphase, anaphase, and telophase. ("Mitophase" is not one of the steps.) During prophase, the cell begins the nonstop process of division. Its chromatin condenses, its nucleolus disappears, the nuclear membrane breaks apart, mitotic spindles form, its cytoskeleton breaks down, and centrioles push the spindles apart. Note that interphase, the stage where chromatin is loose, chromosomes are replicated, and cell metabolism is occurring, is technically not a stage of mitosis; it is a precursor to cell division.

19. The Doppler Effect is associated most closely with which property of waves?

A. Amplitude.

B. Wavelength.

C. Frequency.

D. Intensity.

C. Frequency.

The Doppler Effect accounts for an apparent increase in frequency when a wave source moves toward a wave receiver or apparent decrease in frequency when a wave source moves away from a wave receiver. (Note that the receiver could also be moving toward or away from the source.) As the wave fronts are released, motion toward the receiver mimics more frequent wave fronts, while motion away from the receiver mimics less frequent wave fronts. Meanwhile, the amplitude, wavelength, and intensity of the wave are not as relevant to this process (although moving closer to a wave source makes it seem more intense). The **answer to this question is therefore (C)**.

20. Viruses are responsible for many human diseases including all of the following *except*

A. influenza.

B. A.I.D.S.

C. the common cold.

D. strep throat.

D. Strep throat.

Influenza, A.I.D.S., and the "common cold" (rhinovirus infection), are all caused by viruses. (This is the reason that doctors should not be pressured to prescribe antibiotics for colds or 'flu—i.e. they will not be effective since the infections are not bacterial.) Strep throat (properly called 'streptococcal throat' and caused by streptococcus bacteria) is not a virus, but a bacterial infection. Thus, the **answer is (D)**.

21. A series of experiments on pea plants formed by _____ showed that two invisible markers existed for each trait, and one marker dominated the other.

A. Pasteur.

B. Watson and Crick.

C. Mendel.

D. Mendeleev.

C. Mendel.

Gregor Mendel was a ninteenth-century Austrian botanist, who derived "laws" governing inherited traits. His work led to the understanding of dominant and recessive traits, carried by biological markers. Mendel cross-bred different kinds of pea plants with varying features and observed the resulting new plants. He showed that genetic characteristics are not passed identically from one generation to the next. (Pasteur, Watson, Crick, and Mendeleev were other scientists with different specialties.) This is consistent only with **answer (C)**.

22. Formaldehyde should not be used in school laboratories for the following reason:

A. it smells unpleasant.

B. it is a known carcinogen.

C. it is expensive to obtain.

D. it is an explosive.

B. It is a known carcinogen.

Formaldehyde is a known carcinogen, so it is too dangerous for use in schools. In general, teachers should not use carcinogens in school laboratories. Although formaldehyde also smells unpleasant, a smell alone is not a definitive marker of danger. For example, many people find the smell of vinegar to be unpleasant, but vinegar is considered a very safe classroom/laboratory chemical. Furthermore, some odorless materials are toxic. Formaldehyde is neither particularly expensive nor explosive. Thus, the **answer is (B)**.

23. Amino acids are carried to the ribosome in protein synthesis by:

A. transfer RNA (tRNA).

B. messenger RNA (mRNA).

C. ribosomal RNA (rRNA).

D. transformation RNA (trRNA).

A. Transfer RNA (tRNA).

The job of tRNA is to carry and position amino acids to/on the ribosomes. mRNA copies DNA code and brings it to the ribosomes; rRNA is in the ribosome itself. There is no such thing as trRNA. Thus, the **answer is (A)**.

24. When designing a scientific experiment, a student considers all the factors that may influence the results. The process goal is to _____

A. recognize and manipulate independent variables.

B. recognize and record independent variables.

C. recognize and manipulate dependent variables.

D. recognize and record dependent variables.

A. Recognize and manipulate independent variables.

When a student designs a scientific experiment, s/he must decide what to measure, and what independent variables will play a role in the experiment. S/he must determine how to manipulate these independent variables to refine his/her procedure and to prepare for meaningful observations. Although s/he will eventually record dependent variables (D), this does not take place during the experimental design phase. Although the student will likely recognize and record the independent variables (B), this is not the process goal, but a helpful step in manipulating the variables. It is unlikely that the student will manipulate dependent variables directly in his/her experiment (C), or the data would be suspect. Thus, the **answer is (A)**.

25. Since ancient times, people have been entranced with bird flight. What is the key to bird flight?

A. Bird wings are a particular shape and composition.

B. Birds flap their wings quickly enough to propel themselves.

C. Birds take advantage of tailwinds.

D. Birds take advantage of crosswinds.

A. Bird wings are a particular shape and composition.

Bird wings are shaped for wide area, and their bones are very light. This creates a large surface-area-to-mass ratio, enabling birds to glide in air. Birds do flap their wings and float on winds, but none of these is the main reason for their flight ability. Thus, the **answer is (A)**.

26. Laboratory researchers have classified fungi as distinct from plants because the cell walls of fungi

A. contain chitin.

B. contain yeast.

C. are more solid.

D. are less solid.

A. Contain chitin.

Kingdom Fungi consists of organisms that are eukaryotic, multicellular, absorptive consumers. They have a chitin cell wall, which is the only universally present feature in fungi that is never present in plants. Thus, the **answer is (A)**.

27. In a fission reactor, "heavy water" is used to _____

A. terminate fission reactions.

B. slow down neutrons and moderate reactions.

C. rehydrate the chemicals.

D. initiate a chain reaction.

B. Slow down neutrons and moderate reactions.

"Heavy water" is used in a nuclear [fission] reactor to slow down neutrons, controlling and moderating the nuclear reactions. It does not terminate the reaction, and it does not initiate the reaction. Also, although the reactor takes advantage of water's other properties (e.g. high specific heat for cooling), the water does not "rehydrate" the chemicals. Therefore, the **answer is (B)**.

28. The transfer of heat by electromagnetic waves is called _____

A. conduction.

B. convection.

C. phase change.

D. radiation.

D. Radiation.

Heat transfer via electromagnetic waves (which can occur even in a vacuum) is called radiation. (Heat can also be transferred by direct contact (conduction), by fluid current (convection), and by matter changing phase, but these are not relevant here.) The answer to this question is **therefore (D)**.

29. When heat is added to most solids, they expand. Why is this the case?

A. The molecules get bigger.

B. The faster molecular motion leads to greater distance between the molecules.

C. The molecules develop greater repelling electric forces.

D. The molecules form a more rigid structure.

B. The faster molecular motion leads to greater distance between the molecules.

The atomic theory of matter states that matter is made up of tiny, rapidly moving particles. These particles move more quickly when warmer, because temperature is a measure of average kinetic energy of the particles. Warmer molecules therefore move further away from each other, with enough energy to separate from each other more often and for greater distances. The individual molecules do not get bigger, by conservation of mass, eliminating answer (A). The molecules do not develop greater repelling electric forces, eliminating answer (C). Occasionally, molecules form a more rigid structure when becoming colder and freezing (such as water)—but this gives rise to the exceptions to heat expansion, so it is not relevant here, eliminating answer (D). Therefore, the **answer is (B)**.

30. The force of gravity on earth causes all bodies in free fall to _____

A. fall at the same speed.

B. accelerate at the same rate.

C. reach the same terminal velocity.

D. move in the same direction.

B. Accelerate at the same rate.

Gravity causes approximately the same acceleration on all falling bodies close to earth's surface. (It is only "approximately" because there are very small variations in the strength of earth's gravitational field.) More massive bodies continue to accelerate at this rate for longer, before their air resistance is great enough to cause terminal velocity, so answers (A) and (C) are eliminated. Bodies on different parts of the planet move in different directions (always toward the center of mass of earth), so answer (D) is eliminated. Thus, the **answer is (B)**.

31. Sound waves are produced by _____

A. pitch.

B. noise.

C. vibrations.

D. sonar.

C. Vibrations.

Sound waves are produced by a vibrating body. The vibrating object moves forward and compresses the air in front of it, then reverses direction so that the pressure on the air is lessened and expansion of the air molecules occurs. The vibrating air molecules move back and forth parallel to the direction of motion of the wave as they pass the energy from adjacent air molecules closer to the source to air molecules farther away from the source. Therefore, the **answer is (C)**.

32. Resistance is measured in units called

A. watts.

B. volts.

C. ohms.

D. current.

C. Ohms.

A watt is a unit of energy. Potential difference is measured in a unit called the volt. Current is the number of electrons per second that flow past a point in a circuit. An ohm is the unit for resistance. The correct **answer is (C).**

33. Sound can be transmitted in all of the following *except*

A. air.

B. water.

C. diamond.

D. a vacuum.

D. A vacuum.

Sound, a longitudinal wave, is transmitted by vibrations of molecules. Therefore, it can be transmitted through any gas, liquid, or solid. However, it cannot be transmitted through a vacuum, because there are no particles present to vibrate and bump into their adjacent particles to transmit the waves. This is consistent only with **answer (D)**. (It is interesting also to note that sound is actually faster in solids and liquids than in air.)

34. As a train approaches, the whistle sounds

A. higher, because it has a higher apparent frequency.

B. lower, because it has a lower apparent frequency.

C. higher, because it has a lower apparent frequency.

D. lower, because it has a higher apparent frequency.

A. Higher, because it has a higher apparent frequency.

By the Doppler effect, when a source of sound is moving toward an observer, the wave fronts are released closer together, i.e. with a greater apparent frequency. Higher frequency sounds are higher in pitch. This is consistent only with **answer (A)**.

35. The speed of light is different in different materials. This is responsible for _____

A. interference.

B. refraction.

C. reflection.

D. relativity.

B. Refraction.

Refraction (B) is the bending of light because it hits a material at an angle wherein it has a different speed. (This is analogous to a cart rolling on a smooth road. If it hits a rough patch at an angle, the wheel on the rough patch slows down first, leading to a change in direction.) Interference (A) is when light waves interfere with each other to form brighter or dimmer patterns; reflection (C) is when light bounces off a surface; relativity (D) is a general topic related to light speed and its implications, but not specifically indicated here. Therefore, the **answer is (B)**.

36. A converging lens produces a real image _____

A. always.

B. never.

C. when the object is within one focal length of the lens.

D. when the object is further than one focal length from the lens.

D. When the object is further than one focal length from the lens.

A converging lens produces a real image whenever the object is far enough from the lens (outside one focal length) so that the rays of light from the object can hit the lens and be focused into a real image on the other side of the lens. When the object is closer than one focal length from the lens, rays of light do not converge on the other side; they diverge. This means that only a virtual image can be formed, i.e. the theoretical place where those diverging rays would have converged if they had originated behind the object. Thus, the correct **answer is (D)**.

37. The electromagnetic radiation with the longest wave length is/are

_____

A. radio waves.

B. red light.

C. X-rays.

D. ultraviolet light.

A. Radio waves.

As one can see on a diagram of the electromagnetic spectrum, radio waves have longer wave lengths (and smaller frequencies) than visible light, which in turn has longer wave lengths than ultraviolet or X-ray radiation. If you did not remember this sequence, you might recall that wave length is inversely proportional to frequency, and that radio waves are considered much less harmful (less energetic, i.e. lower frequency) than ultraviolet or X-ray radiation. The correct answer is **therefore (A)**.

38. Under a 440 power microscope, an object with diameter 0.1 millimeter appears to have diameter _____

A. 4.4 millimeters.

B. 44 millimeters.

C. 440 millimeters.

D. 4400 millimeters.

B. 44 millimeters.

To answer this question, recall that to calculate a new length, you multiply the original length by the magnification power of the instrument. Therefore, the 0.1 millimeter diameter is multiplied by 440. This equals 44, so the image appears to be 44 millimeters in diameter. You could also reason that since a 440 power microscope is considered a "high power" microscope, you would expect a 0.1 millimeter object to appear a few centimeters long. Therefore, the correct **answer is (B).**

39. To separate blood into blood cells and plasma involves the process of

A. electrophoresis.

B. spectrophotometry.

C. centrifugation.

D. chromatography.

C. Centrifugation.

Electrophoresis uses electrical charges of molecules to separate them according to their size. Spectrophotometry uses percent light absorbance to measure a color change, thus giving qualitative data a quantitative value. Chromatography uses the principles of capillarity to separate substances. Centrifugation involves spinning substances at a high speed. The more dense part of a solution will settle to the bottom of the test tube, where the lighter material will stay on top. The **answer is (C).**

40. Experiments may be done with any of the following animals except

A. birds.

B. invertebrates.

C .lower order life.

D. frogs.

A. Birds.

No dissections may be performed on living mammalian vertebrates or birds. Lower order life and invertebrates may be used. Biological experiments may be done with all animals except mammalian vertebrates or birds. Therefore the **answer is (A).**

41. For her first project of the year, a student is designing a science experiment to test the effects of light and water on plant growth. You should recommend that she _____

A. manipulate the temperature also.

B. manipulate the water pH also.

C. determine the relationship between light and water unrelated to plant growth.

D. omit either water or light as a variable.

D. Omit either water or light as a variable.

As a science teacher for middle-school-aged kids, it is important to reinforce the idea of 'constant' vs. 'variable' in science experiments. At this level, it is wisest to have only one variable examined in each science experiment. (Later, students can hold different variables constant while investigating others.) Therefore it is counterproductive to add in other variables (answers (A)or (B)). It is also irrelevant to determine the light-water interactions aside from plant growth (C). So the only possible **answer is (D)**.

42. In a laboratory report, what is the abstract?

A. The abstract is a summary of the report, and is the first section of the report.

B. The abstract is a summary of the report, and is the last section of the report.

C. The abstract is predictions for future experiments, and is the first section of the report.

D. The abstract is predictions for future experiments, and is the last section of the report.

A. The abstract is a summary of the report, and is the first section of the report.

In a laboratory report, the abstract is the section that summarizes the entire report (often containing one representative sentence from each section). It appears at the very beginning of the report, even before the introduction, often on its own page (instead of a title page). This format is consistent with articles in scientific journals. Therefore, the **answer is (A).**

43. What is the scientific method?

A. It is the process of doing an experiment and writing a laboratory report.

B. It is the process of using open inquiry and repeatable results to establish theories.

C. It is the process of reinforcing scientific principles by confirming results.

D. It is the process of recording data and observations.

B. It is the process of using open inquiry and repeatable results to establish theories.

Scientific research often includes elements from answers (A), (C), and (D), but the basic underlying principle of the scientific method is that people ask questions and do repeatable experiments to answer those questions and develop informed theories of why and how things happen. Therefore, the best **answer is (B).**

44. Identify the control in the following experiment: A student had four corn plants and was measuring photosynthetic rate (by measuring growth mass). Half of the plants were exposed to full (constant) sunlight, and the other half were kept in 50% (constant) sunlight.

A. The control is a set of plants grown in full (constant) sunlight.

B. The control is a set of plants grown in 50% (constant) sunlight.

C. The control is a set of plants grown in the dark.

D. The control is a set of plants grown in a mixture of natural levels of sunlight.

A. The control is a set of plants grown in full (constant) sunlight.

In this experiment, the goal was to measure how two different amounts of sunlight affected plant growth. The control in any experiment is the 'base case,' or the usual situation without a change in variable. Because the control must be studied alongside the variable, answers (C) and (D) are omitted (because they were not in the experiment). The **better answer of (A) and (B) is (A)**, because usually plants are assumed to have the best growth and their usual growing circumstances in full sunlight. This is particularly true for crops like the corn plants in this question.

45. In an experiment measuring the growth of bacteria at different temperatures, what is the independent variable?

A. Number of bacteria.

B. Growth rate of bacteria.

C. Temperature.

D. Light intensity.

C. Temperature.

To answer this question, recall that the independent variable in an experiment is the entity that is changed by the scientist, in order to observe the effects (the dependent variable(s)). In this experiment, temperature is changed in order to measure growth of bacteria, so **(C) is the answer**. Note that answer (A) is the dependent variable, and neither (B) nor (D) is directly relevant to the question.

46. A scientific law _____

A. proves scientific accuracy.

B. may never be broken.

C. may be revised in light of new data.

D. is the result of one excellent experiment.

C. May be revised in light of new data.

A scientific law is the same as a scientific theory, except that it has lasted for longer, and has been supported by more extensive data. Therefore, such a law may be revised in light of new data, and may be broken by that new data. Furthermore, a scientific law is always the result of many experiments, and never 'proves' anything but rather is implied or supported by various results. Therefore, the **answer must be (C).**

47. Which is the correct order of methodology?

1. collecting data
2. planning a controlled experiment
3. drawing a conclusion
4. hypothesizing a result
5. re-visiting a hypothesis to answer a question

A. 1,2,3,4,5

B. 4,2,1,3,5

C. 4,5,1,3,2

D. 1,3,4,5,2

B. 4,2,1,3,5

The correct methodology for the scientific method is first to make a meaningful hypothesis (educated guess), then plan and execute a controlled experiment to test that hypothesis. Using the data collected in that experiment, the scientist then draws conclusions and attempts to answer the original question related to the hypothesis. This is consistent only with **answer (B).**

48. Which is the most desirable tool to use to heat substances in a middle school laboratory?

A. Alcohol burner.

B. Freestanding gas burner.

C. Bunsen burner.

D. Hot plate.

D. Hot plate.

Due to safety considerations, the use of open flame should be minimized, so a hot plate is the best choice. Any kind of burner may be used with proper precautions, but it is difficult to maintain a completely safe middle school environment. Therefore, the best **answer is (D)**.

49. Newton's Laws are taught in science classes because _____.

A. they are the correct analysis of inertia, gravity, and forces.

B. they are a close approximation to correct physics, for usual Earth conditions.

C. they accurately incorporate Relativity into studies of forces.

D. Newton was a well-respected scientist in his time.

They are a close approximation to correct physics, for usual Earth conditions.

Although Newton's Laws are often taught as fully correct for inertia, gravity, and forces, it is important to realize that Einstein's work (and that of others) has indicated that Newton's Laws are reliable only at speeds much lower than that of light. This is reasonable, though, for most middle- and high-school applications. At speeds close to the speed of light, Relativity considerations must be used. Therefore, the only correct **answer is (B)**.

50. Which of the following is most accurate?

A. Mass is always constant; Weight may vary by location.

B. Mass and Weight are both always constant.

C. Weight is always constant; Mass may vary by location.

D. Mass and Weight may both vary by location.

A. Mass is always constant; Weight may vary by location.

When considering situations exclusive of nuclear reactions, mass is constant (mass, the amount of matter in a system, is conserved). Weight, on the other hand, is the force of gravity on an object, which is subject to change due to changes in the gravitational field and/or the location of the object. Thus, the **best answer is (A)**.

51. Chemicals should be stored _____

A. in the principal's office.

B. in a dark room.

C. in an off-site research facility.

D. according to their reactivity with other substances.

D. According to their reactivity with other substances.

Chemicals should be stored with other chemicals of similar properties (e.g. acids with other acids), to reduce the potential for either hazardous reactions in the storeroom, or mistakes in reagent use. Certainly, chemicals should not be stored in anyone's office, and the light intensity of the room is not very important because light-sensitive chemicals are usually stored in dark containers. In fact, good lighting is desirable in a storeroom, so that labels can be read easily. Chemicals may be stored off-site, but that makes their use inconvenient. Therefore, the best **answer is (D)**.

52. Which of the following is the worst choice for a school laboratory activity?

A. A genetics experiment tracking the fur color of mice.

B. Dissection of a preserved fetal pig.

C. Measurement of goldfish respiration rate at different temperatures.

D. Pithing a frog to watch the circulatory system.

D. Pithing a frog to watch the circulatory system.

While any use of animals (alive or dead) must be done with care to respect ethics and laws, it is possible to perform choices (A), (B), or (C) with due care. (Note that students will need significant assistance and maturity to perform these experiments.) However, modern practice precludes pithing animals (causing partial brain death while allowing some systems to function), as inhumane. Therefore, the answer to this **question is (D)**.

53. Who should be notified in the case of a serious chemical spill?

A. The custodian.

B. The fire department or other municipal authority.

C. The science department chair.

D. The School Board.

B. The fire department or other municipal authority.

Although the custodian may help to clean up laboratory messes, and the science department chair should be involved in discussions of ways to avoid spills, a serious chemical spill may require action by the fire department or other trained emergency personnel. It is best to be safe by notifying them in case of a serious chemical accident. Therefore, the **best answer is (B)**.

54. A scientist exposes mice to cigarette smoke, and notes that their lungs develop tumors. Mice that were not exposed to the smoke do not develop as many tumors. Which of the following conclusions may be drawn from these results?

I. Cigarette smoke causes lung tumors.
II. Cigarette smoke exposure has a positive correlation with lung tumors in mice.
III. Some mice are predisposed to develop lung tumors.
IV. Mice are often a good model for humans in scientific research.

A. I and II only.

B. II only.

C. I , II, and III only.

D. II and IV only.

B. II only.

Although cigarette smoke has been found to cause lung tumors (and many other problems), this particular experiment shows only that there is a positive correlation between smoke exposure and tumor development in these mice. It may be true that some mice are more likely to develop tumors than others, which is why a control group of identical mice should have been used for comparison. Mice are often used to model human reactions, but this is as much due to their low financial and emotional cost as it is due to their being a "good model" for humans. Therefore, the **answer must be (B)**.

55. In which situation would a science teacher be legally liable?

A. The teacher leaves the classroom for a telephone call and a student slips and injures him/herself.

B. A student removes his/her goggles and gets acid in his/her eye.

C. A faulty gas line in the classroom causes a fire.

D. A student cuts him/herself with a dissection scalpel.

The teacher leaves the classroom for a telephone call and a student slips and injures him/herself.

Teachers are required to exercise a "reasonable duty of care" for their students. Accidents may happen (D), or students may make poor decisions (B), or facilities may break down (C). However, the teacher has the responsibility to be present and to do his/her best to create a safe and effective learning environment. Therefore, the **answer is (A)**.

56. Which of these is the best example of 'negligence'?

A. A teacher fails to give oral instructions to those with reading disabilities.

B. A teacher fails to exercise ordinary care to ensure safety in the classroom.

C. A teacher displays inability to supervise a large group of students.

D. A teacher reasonably anticipates that an event may occur, and plans accordingly.

A teacher fails to exercise ordinary care to ensure safety in the classroom.

'Negligence' is the failure to "exercise ordinary care" to ensure an appropriate and safe classroom environment. It is best for a teacher to meet all special requirements for disabled students, and to be good at supervising large groups. However, if a teacher can prove that s/he has done a reasonable job to ensure a safe and effective learning environment, then it is unlikely that she/he would be found negligent. Therefore, **the answer is (B)**.

57. Which item should always be used when handling glassware?

A. Tongs.

B. Safety goggles.

C. Gloves.

D. Buret stand.

B. Safety goggles.

Safety goggles are the single most important piece of safety equipment in the laboratory, and should be used any time a scientist is using glassware, heat, or chemicals. Other equipment (e.g. tongs, gloves, or even a buret stand) has its place for various applications. However, the most important is safety goggles. Therefore, the **answer is (B)**.

58. Which of the following is *not* a necessary characteristic of living things?

A. Movement.

B. Reduction of local entropy.

C. Ability to cause local energy form changes.

D. Reproduction.

A. Movement.

There are many definitions of "life," but in all cases, a living organism reduces local entropy, changes chemical energy into other forms, and reproduces. Not all living things move, however, so the correct **answer is (A)**.

59. What are the most significant and prevalent elements in the biosphere?

A. Carbon, Hydrogen, Oxygen, Nitrogen, Phosphorus.

B. Carbon, Hydrogen, Sodium, Iron, Calcium.

C. Carbon, Oxygen, Sulfur, Manganese, Iron.

D. Carbon, Hydrogen, Oxygen, Nickel, Sodium, Nitrogen.

A. Carbon, Hydrogen, Oxygen, Nitrogen, Phosphorus.
Organic matter (and life as we know it) is based on carbon atoms, bonded to hydrogen and oxygen. Nitrogen and phosphorus are the next most significant elements, followed by sulfur and then trace nutrients such as iron, sodium, calcium, and others. Therefore, the **answer is (A)**. If you know that the formula for any carbohydrate contains carbon, hydrogen, and Oxygen, that will help you narrow the choices to (A) and (D) in any case.

60. All of the following measure energy *except* for _____

A. joules.

B. calories.

C. watts.

D. ergs.

C. Watts.

Energy units must be dimensionally equivalent to (force)x(length), which equals (mass)x(length squared)/(time squared). Joules, Calories, and ergs are all metric measures of energy. Joules are the SI units of energy, while Calories are used to allow water to have a specific heat of one unit. Ergs are used in the 'cgs' (centimeter-gram-second) system, for smaller quantities. Watts, however, are units of power, i.e. joules per second. Therefore, the **answer is (C)**.

61. Identify the correct sequence of organization of living things from lower to higher order:

A. Cell, Organelle, Organ, Tissue, System, Organism.

B. Cell, Tissue, Organ, Organelle, System, Organism.

C. Organelle, Cell, Tissue, Organ, System, Organism.

D. Organelle, Tissue, Cell, Organ, System, Organism.

C. Organelle, Cell, Tissue, Organ, System, Organism.

Organelles are parts of the cell; cells make up tissue, which makes up organs. Organs work together in systems (e.g. the respiratory system), and the organism is the living thing as a whole. Therefore, the **answer must be (C)**.

62. Which kingdom is comprised of organisms made of one cell with no nuclear membrane?

A. Monera.

B. Protista.

C. Fungi.

D. Algae.

A. Monera.

To answer this question, first note that algae are not a kingdom of their own. Some algae are in Monera, the kingdom that consists of unicellular prokaryotes with no true nucleus. Protista and fungi are both eukaryotic, with true nuclei, and are sometimes multicellular. Therefore, the **answer is (A)**.

63. Which of the following is found in the least abundance in organic molecules?

A. Phosphorus.

B. Potassium.

C. Carbon.

D. Oxygen.

B. Potassium.

Organic molecules consist mainly of carbon, hydrogen, and oxygen, with significant amounts of nitrogen, phosphorus, and often sulfur. Other elements, such as potassium, are present in much smaller quantities. Therefore, the **answer is (B)**. If you were not aware of this ranking, you might have been able to eliminate carbon and oxygen because of their prevalence, in any case.

64. Catalysts assist reactions by _____

A. lowering effective activation energy.

B. maintaining precise pH levels.

C. keeping systems at equilibrium.

D. adjusting reaction speed.

A. Lowering effective activation energy.

Chemical reactions can be enhanced or accelerated by catalysts, which are present both with reactants and with products. They induce the formation of activated complexes, thereby lowering the effective activation energy—so that less energy is necessary for the reaction to begin. Although this often makes reactions faster, answer (D) is not as good a choice as the more generally applicable **answer (A)**, which is correct.

65. Accepted procedures for preparing solutions should be made with

A. alcohol.

B. hydrochloric acid.

C. distilled water.

D. tap water.

C. Distilled water.

Alcohol and hydrochloric acid should never be used to make solutions unless instructed to do so. All solutions should be made with distilled water as tap water contains dissolved particles which may affect the results of an experiment. The correct **answer is (C).**

66. Enzymes speed up reactions by _____

A. utilizing ATP.

B. lowering pH, allowing reaction speed to increase.

C. increasing volume of substrate.

D. lowering energy of activation.

D. Lowering energy of activation.

Because enzymes are catalysts, they work the same way—they cause the formation of activated chemical complexes, which require a lower activation energy. Therefore, the **answer is (D).** ATP is an energy source for cells, and pH or volume changes may or may not affect reaction rate, so these answers can be eliminated.

67. When you step out of the shower, the floor feels colder on your feet than the bathmat. Which of the following is the correct explanation for this phenomenon?

A. The floor is colder than the bathmat.

B. Your feet have a chemical reaction with the floor, but not the bathmat.

C. Heat is conducted more easily into the floor.

D. Water is absorbed from your feet into the bathmat.

C. Heat is conducted more easily into the floor.

When you step out of the shower and onto a surface, the surface is most likely at room temperature, regardless of its composition eliminating answer (A). Your feet feel cold when heat is transferred from them to the surface, which happens more easily on a hard floor than a soft bathmat. This is because of differences in specific heat (the energy required to change temperature, which varies by material). Therefore, the **answer must be (C)**,

68. Which of the following is *not* considered ethical behavior for a scientist?

A. Using unpublished data and citing the source.

B. Publishing data before other scientists have had a chance to replicate results.

C. Collaborating with other scientists from different laboratories.

D. Publishing work with an incomplete list of citations.

D. Publishing work with an incomplete list of citations.

One of the most important ethical principles for scientists is to cite all sources of data and analysis when publishing work. It is reasonable to use unpublished data (A), as long as the source is cited. Most science is published before other scientists replicate it (B), and frequently scientists collaborate with each other, in the same or different laboratories (C). These are all ethical choices. However, publishing work without the appropriate citations is unethical. Therefore, the **answer is (D).**

69. The chemical equation for water formation is: $2H_2 + O_2 \rightarrow 2H_2O$. Which of the following is an *incorrect* interpretation of this equation?

A. Two moles of hydrogen gas and one mole of oxygen gas combine to make two moles of water.

B. Two grams of hydrogen gas and one gram of oxygen gas combine to make two grams of water.

C. Two molecules of hydrogen gas and one molecule of oxygen gas combine to make two molecules of water.

D. Four atoms of hydrogen (combined as a diatomic gas) and two atoms of oxygen (combined as a diatomic gas) combine to make two molecules of water.

B. Two grams of hydrogen gas and one gram of oxygen gas combine to make two grams of water.

In any chemical equation, the coefficients indicate the relative proportions of molecules (or atoms), or of moles of molecules. They do not refer to mass, because chemicals combine in repeatable combinations of molar ratio (i.e. number of moles), but vary in mass per mole of material. Therefore, the answer must be the only choice that does not refer to numbers of particles, **answer (B)**, which refers to grams, a unit of mass.

70. Energy is measured with the same units as _____

A. force.

B. momentum.

C. work.

D. power.

C. Work.

In SI units, energy is measured in Joules, i.e. (mass)(length squared)/(time squared). This is the same unit as is used for work. You can verify this by calculating that since work is force times distance, the units work out to be the same. Force is measured in Newtons in SI; momentum is measured in (mass)(length)/(time); power is measured in Watts (which equal Joules/second). Therefore, the **answer must be (C)**.

71. If the volume of a confined gas is increased, what happens to the pressure of the gas? You may assume that the gas behaves ideally, and that temperature and number of gas molecules remain constant.

A. The pressure increases.

B. The pressure decreases.

C. The pressure stays the same.

D. There is not enough information given to answer this question.

B. The pressure decreases.

Because we are told that the gas behaves ideally, you may assume that it follows the Ideal Gas Law, i.e. PV = nRT. This means that an increase in volume must be associated with a decrease in pressure (i.e. higher V means lower P), because we are also given that all the components of the right side of the equation remain constant. Therefore, the **answer must be (B)**.

72. A product of anaerobic respiration in animals is _____

A. carbon dioxide.

B. lactic acid.

C. oxygen.

D. sodium chloride.

B. Lactic acid.

In animals, anaerobic respiration (i.e. respiration without the presence of oxygen) generates lactic acid as a byproduct. (Note that some anaerobic bacteria generate carbon dioxide from respiration of methane, and animals generate carbon dioxide in aerobic respiration.) Oxygen is not normally a by-product of respiration, though it is a product of photosynthesis, and sodium chloride is not strictly relevant in this question. Therefore, the **answer must be (B)**. By the way, lactic acid is believed to cause muscle soreness after anaerobic weight-lifting.

73. A Newton is fundamentally a measure of _____.

A. force.

B. momentum.

C. energy.

D. gravity.

A. Force.

In SI units, force is measured in Newtons. Momentum and energy each have different units, without equivalent dimensions. A Newton is one (kilogram)(meter)/(second squared), while momentum is measured in (kilgram)(meter)/(second) and energy, in Joules, is (kilogram)(meter squared)/(second squared). Although "gravity" can be interpreted as the force of gravity, i.e. measured in Newtons, fundamentally it is not required. Therefore, the **answer is (A)**.

74. Which change does *not* affect enzyme rate?

A. Increase the temperature.

B. Add more substrate.

C. Adjust the pH.

D. Use a larger cell.

D. Use a larger cell.

Temperature, chemical amounts, and pH can all affect enzyme rate. However, the chemical reactions take place on a small enough scale that the overall cell size is not relevant. Therefore, the **answer is (D)**.

75. Which of the following types of rock are made from magma?

A. Fossils.

B. Sedimentary.

C. Metamorphic.

D. Igneous.

D. Igneous.

Few fossils are found in metamorphic rock and virtually none found in igneous rocks. Igneous rocks are formed from magma and magma is so hot that any organisms trapped by it are destroyed. Metamorphic rocks are formed by high temperatures and great pressures. When fluid sediments are transformed into solid sedimentary rocks, the process is known as lithification. The **answer is (D).**

76. Which of the following is _not_ an acceptable way for a student to acknowledge sources in a laboratory report?

A. The student tells his/her teacher what sources s/he used to write the report.

B. The student uses footnotes in the text, with sources cited, but not in correct MLA format.

C. The student uses endnotes in the text, with sources cited, in correct MLA format.

D. The student attaches a separate bibliography, noting each use of sources.

A. The student tells his/her teacher what sources s/he used to write the report.

It may seem obvious, but students are often unaware that scientists need to cite all sources used. For the young adolescent, it is not always necessary to use official MLA format (though this should be taught at some point). Students may properly cite references in many ways, but these references must be in writing, with the original assignment. Therefore, the **answer is (A).**

77. Animals with a notochord or a backbone are in the phylum

A. Arthropoda.

B. Chordata.

C. Mollusca.

D. Mammalia.

B. Chordata.

The phylum Arthropoda contains spiders and insects and phylum Mollusca contain snails and squid. Mammalia is a class in the phylum Chordata. The **answer is (B).**

78. Which of the following is a correct explanation for scientific 'evolution'?

A. Giraffes need to reach higher for leaves to eat, so their necks stretch. The giraffe babies are then born with longer necks. Eventually, there are more long-necked giraffes in the population.

B. Giraffes with longer necks are able to reach more leaves, so they eat more and have more babies than other giraffes. Eventually, there are more long-necked giraffes in the population.

C. Giraffes want to reach higher for leaves to eat, so they release enzymes into their bloodstream, which in turn causes fetal development of longer-necked giraffes. Eventually, there are more long-necked giraffes in the population.

D. Giraffes with long necks are more attractive to other giraffes, so they get the best mating partners and have more babies. Eventually, there are more long-necked giraffes in the population.

B. Giraffes with longer necks are able to reach more leaves, so they eat more and have more babies than other giraffes. Eventually, there are more long-necked giraffes in the population.

Although evolution is often misunderstood, it occurs via natural selection. Organisms with a survival/reproductive advantage will produce more offspring. Over many generations, this changes the proportions of the population. In any case, it is impossible for a stretched neck (A) or a fervent desire (C) to result in a biologically mutated baby. Although there are traits that are naturally selected because of mate attractiveness and fitness (D), this is not the primary situation here, **so answer (B) is the best choice.**

79. Which of the following is a correct definition for 'chemical equilibrium'?

A. Chemical equilibrium is when the forward and backward reaction rates are equal. The reaction may continue to proceed forward and backward.

B. Chemical equilibrium is when the forward and backward reaction rates are equal, and equal to zero. The reaction does not continue.

C. Chemical equilibrium is when there are equal quantities of reactants and products.

D. Chemical equilibrium is when acids and bases neutralize each other fully.

A. Chemical equilibrium is when the forward and backward reaction rates are equal. The reaction may continue to proceed forward and backward.

Chemical equilibrium is defined as when the quantities of reactants and products are at a 'steady state' and are no longer shifting, but the reaction may still proceed forward and backward. The rate of forward reaction must equal the rate of backward reaction. Note that there may or may not be equal amounts of chemicals, and that this is not restricted to a completed reaction or to an acid-base reaction. Therefore, the **answer is (A)**.

80. Which of the following data sets is properly represented by a bar graph?

A. Number of people choosing to buy cars, vs. Color of car bought.

B. Number of people choosing to buy cars, vs. Age of car customer.

C. Number of people choosing to buy cars, vs. Distance from car lot to customer home.

D. Number of people choosing to buy cars, vs. Time since last car purchase.

A. Number of people choosing to buy cars, vs. Color of car bought.

A bar graph should be used only for data sets in which the independent variable is non-continuous (discrete), ie. gender, color, etc. Any continuous independent variable (age, distance, time, etc.) should yield a scatter-plot when the dependent variable is plotted. Therefore, the **answer must be (A)**.

81. In a science experiment, a student needs to dispense very small measured amounts of liquid into a well-mixed solution. Which of the following is the best choice for his/her equipment to use?

A. Buret with Buret Stand, Stir-plate, Stirring Rod, Beaker.

B. Buret with Buret Stand, Stir-plate, Beaker.

C. Volumetric Flask, Dropper, Graduated Cylinder, Stirring Rod.

D. Beaker, Graduated Cylinder, Stir-plate.

B. Buret with Buret Stand, Stir-plate, Beaker.

The most accurate and convenient way to dispense small measured amounts of liquid in the laboratory is with a buret, on a buret stand. To keep a solution well-mixed, a magnetic stir-plate is the most sensible choice, and the solution will usually be mixed in a beaker. Although other combinations of materials could be used for this experiment, **choice (B)** is thus the simplest and best.

82. A laboratory balance is most appropriately used to measure the mass of which of the following?

A. Seven paper clips.

B. Three oranges.

C. Two hundred cells.

D. One student's elbow.

A. Seven paper clips.

Usually, laboratory/classroom balances can measure masses between approximately 0.01 gram and 100 grams. Therefore, answer (B) is too heavy and answer (C) is too light. Answer (D) is silly, but it is a reminder to instruct students not to lean on the balances or put their things near them. **Answer (A)**, which is likely to have a mass of a few grams, is correct in this case.

83. All of the following are measured in units of length, *except* for:

A. Perimeter.

B. Distance.

C. Radius.

D. Area.

D. Area.

Perimeter is the distance around a shape; distance is equivalent to length; radius is the distance from the center (e.g. in a circle) to the edge. Area, however, is the squared-length-units measure of the size of a two-dimensional surface. Therefore, **the answer is (D)**.

84. What is specific gravity?

A. The mass of an object.

B. The ratio of the density of a substance to the density of water.

C. Density.

D. The pull of the earth's gravity on an object.

B. The ratio of the density of a substance to the density of water.

Mass is a measure of the amount of matter in an object. Density is the mass of a substance contained per unit of volume. Weight is the measure of the earth's pull of gravity on an object. The only option here is the ratio of the density of a substance to the density of water, **answer (B)**.

85. What is the most accurate description of the Water Cycle?

A. Rain comes from clouds, filling the ocean. The water then evaporates and becomes clouds again.

B. Water circulates from rivers into groundwater and back, while water vapor circulates in the atmosphere.

C. Water is conserved except for chemical or nuclear reactions, and any drop of water could circulate through clouds, rain, ground-water, and surface-water.

D. Weather systems cause chemical reactions to break water into its atoms.

C. Water is conserved except for chemical or nuclear reactions, and any drop of water could circulate through clouds, rain, ground-water, and surface-water.

All natural chemical cycles, including the Water Cycle, depend on the principle of Conservation of Mass. (For water, unlike for elements such as Nitrogen, chemical reactions may cause sources or sinks of water molecules.) Any drop of water may circulate through the hydrologic system, ending up in a cloud, as rain, or as surface or groundwater. Although answers (A) and (B) describe parts of the water cycle, the most comprehensive and correct **answer is (C)**.

86. The scientific name *Canis familiaris* refers to the animal's _____.

A. kingdom and phylum.

B. genus and species.

C. class and species.

D. type and family.

B. Genus and species.

To answer this question, you must be aware that genus and species are the most specific way to identify an organism, and that usually the genus is capitalized and the species, immediately following, is not. Furthermore, it helps to recall that 'Canis' is the genus for dogs, or canines. Therefore, the **answer must be (B)**. If you did not remember these details, you might recall that there is no such kingdom as 'Canis,' and that there isn't a category 'type' in official taxonomy. This could eliminate answers (A) and (D).

87. Members of the same animal species _____

A. look identical.

B. never adapt differently.

C. are able to reproduce with one another.

D. are found in the same location.

C. Are able to reproduce with one another.

Although members of the same animal species may look alike (A), adapt alike (B), or be found near one another (D), the only requirement is that they be able to reproduce with one another. This ability to reproduce within the group is considered the hallmark of a species. Therefore, the **answer is (C)**.

88. Which of the following is/are true about scientists?

I. Scientists usually work alone.
II. Scientists usually work with other scientists.
III. Scientists achieve more prestige from new discoveries than from replicating established results.
IV. Scientists keep records of their own work, but do not publish it for outside review.

A. I and IV only.

B. II only.

C. II and III only.

D. III and IV only.

C. II and III only.

In the scientific community, scientists nearly always work in teams, both within their institutions and across several institutions. This eliminates (I) and requires (II), leaving only **answer choices (B) and (C)**. Scientists do achieve greater prestige from new discoveries, so the answer must be (C). Note that scientists must publish their work in peer-reviewed journals, eliminating (IV) in any case.

89. What is necessary for ion diffusion to occur spontaneously?

A. Carrier proteins.

B. Energy from an outside source.

C. A concentration gradient.

D. Cell flagella.

C. A concentration gradient.

Spontaneous diffusion occurs when random motion leads particles to increase entropy by equalizing concentrations. Particles tend to move into places of lower concentration. Therefore, a concentration gradient is required, and the **answer is (C)**. No proteins (A), outside energy (B), or flagellae (D) are required for this process.

90. All of the following are considered Newton's Laws *except* for:

A. An object in motion will continue in motion unless acted upon by an outside force.

B. For every action force, there is an equal and opposite reaction force.

C. Nature abhors a vacuum.

D. Mass can be considered the ratio of force to acceleration.

C. Nature abhors a vacuum.

Newton's Laws include his law of inertia (an object in motion (or at rest) will stay in motion (or at rest) until acted upon by an outside force) (A), his law that (Force)=(Mass)(Acceleration) (D), and his equal and opposite reaction force law (B). Therefore, the **answer to this question is (C)**, because "Nature abhors a vacuum" is not one of these.

91. A cup of hot liquid and a cup of cold liquid are both sitting in a room at comfortable room temperature and humidity. Both cups are thin plastic. Which of the following is a true statement?

A. There will be fog on the outside of the hot liquid cup, and also fog on the outside of the cold liquid cup.

B. There will be fog on the outside of the hot liquid cup, but not on the cold liquid cup.

C. There will be fog on the outside of the cold liquid cup, but not on the hot liquid cup.

D. There will not be fog on the outside of either cup.

C. There will be fog on the outside of the cold liquid cup, but not on the hot liquid cup.

Fog forms on the outside of a cup when the contents of the cup are colder than the surrounding air, and the cup material is not a perfect insulator. This happens because the air surrounding the cup is cooled to a lower temperature than the ambient room, so it has a lower saturation point for water vapor. Although the humidity had been reasonable in the warmer air, when that air circulates near the colder region and cools, water condenses onto the cup's outside surface. This phenomenon is also visible when someone takes a hot shower, and the mirror gets foggy. The mirror surface is cooler than the ambient air, and provides a surface for water condensation. Furthermore, the same phenomenon is why defrosters on car windows send heat to the windows—the warmer window does not permit as much condensation. Therefore, the correct **answer is (C)**.

92. A ball rolls down a smooth hill. You may ignore air resistance. Which of the following is a true statement?

A. The ball has more energy at the start of its descent than just before it hits the bottom of the hill, because it is higher up at the beginning.

B. The ball has less energy at the start of its descent than just before it hits the bottom of the hill, because it is moving more quickly at the end.

C. The ball has the same energy throughout its descent, because positional energy is converted to energy of motion.

D. The ball has the same energy throughout its descent, because a single object (such as a ball) cannot gain or lose energy.

The ball has the same energy throughout its descent, because positional energy is converted to energy of motion.

The principle of Conservation of Energy states that (except in cases of nuclear reaction, when energy may be created or destroyed by conversion to mass), "Energy is neither created nor destroyed, but may be transformed." Answers (A) and (B) give you a hint in this question—it is true that the ball has more Potential Energy when it is higher, and that it has more Kinetic Energy when it is moving quickly at the bottom of its descent. However, the total sum of all kinds of energy in the ball remains constant, if we neglect 'losses' to heat/friction. Note that a single object can and does gain or lose energy when the energy is transferred to or from a different object. Conservation of Energy applies to systems, not to individual objects unless they are isolated. Therefore, the **answer must be (C)**.

93. A long silver bar has a temperature of 50 degrees Celsius at one end and 0 degrees Celsius at the other end. The bar will reach thermal equilibrium (barring outside influence) by the process of heat _____.

A. conduction.

B. convection.

C. radiation.

D. phase change.

A. conduction.

Heat conduction is the process of heat transfer via solid contact. The molecules in a warmer region vibrate more rapidly, jostling neighboring molecules and accelerating them. This is the dominant heat transfer process in a solid with no outside influences. Recall, also, that convection is heat transfer by way of fluid currents; radiation is heat transfer via electromagnetic waves; phase change can account for heat transfer in the form of shifts in matter phase. The answer to this question must **therefore be (A)**.

94. _____ are cracks in the plates of the earth's crust, along which the plates move.

A. Faults

B. Ridges

C. Earthquakes

D. Volcanoes

A. Faults.

Faults are cracks in the earth's crust, and when the earth moves, an earthquake results. Faults may lead to mismatched edges of ground, forming ridges, and ground shape may also be determined by volcanoes. The answer to this question must **therefore be (A).**

95. Fossils are usually found in _____ rock.

A. igneous.

B. sedimentary.

C. metamorphic.

D. cumulus.

B. Sedimentary

Fossils are formed by layers of dirt and sand settling around organisms, hardening, and taking an imprint of the organisms. When the organism decays, the hardened imprint is left behind. This is most likely to happen in rocks that form from layers of settling dirt and sand, i.e. sedimentary rock. Note that igneous rock is formed from molten rock from volcanoes (lava), while metamorphic rock can be formed from any rock under very high temperature and pressure changes. 'Cumulus' is a descriptor for clouds, not rocks. The best answer is **therefore (B)**.

96. Which of the following is *not* a common type of acid in 'acid rain' or acidified surface water?

A. Nitric acid.

B. Sulfuric acid.

C. Carbonic acid.

D. Hydrofluoric acid.

D. Hydrofluoric acid.

Acid rain forms predominantly from pollutant oxides in the air (usually nitrogen-based NO_x or sulfur-based SO_x), which become hydrated into their acids (nitric or sulfuric acid). Because of increased levels of carbon dioxide pollution, carbonic acid is also common in acidified surface water environments. Hydrofluoric acid can be found, but it is much less common. In general, carbon, nitrogen, and sulfur are much more prevalent in the environment than fluorine. Therefore, the **answer is (D)**.

97. Which of the following is *not* true about phase change in matter?

A. Solid water and liquid ice can coexist at water's freezing point.

B. At 7 degrees Celsius, water is always in liquid phase.

C. Matter changes phase when enough energy is gained or lost.

D. Different phases of matter are characterized by differences in molecular motion.

B. At 7 degrees Celsius, water is always in liquid phase.

According to the molecular theory of matter, molecular motion determines the 'phase' of the matter, and the energy in the matter determines the speed of molecular motion. Solids have vibrating molecules that are in fixed relative positions; liquids have faster molecular motion than their solid forms, and the molecules may move more freely but must still be in contact with one another; gases have even more energy and more molecular motion. (Other phases, such as plasma, are yet more energetic.) At the 'freezing point' or 'boiling point' of a substance, both relevant phases may be present. For instance, water at zero degrees Celsius may be composed of some liquid and some solid, or all liquid, or all solid. Pressure changes, in addition to temperature changes, can cause phase changes. For example, nitrogen can be liquefied under high pressure, even though its boiling temperature is very low. Therefore, the **correct answer must be (B)**. Water may be a liquid at that temperature, but it may also be a solid, depending on ambient pressure.

98. Which of the following is the longest (largest) unit of geological time?

A. Solar Year.

B. Epoch.

C. Period.

D. Era.

D. Era.

Geological time is measured by many units, but the longest unit listed here (and indeed the longest used to describe the biological development of the planet) is the Era. Eras are subdivided into Periods, which are further divided into Epochs. Therefore, the **answer is (D)**.

99. Extensive use of antibacterial soap has been found to increase the virulence of certain infections in hospitals. Which of the following might be an explanation for this phenomenon?

A. Antibacterial soaps do not kill viruses.

B. Antibacterial soaps do not incorporate the same antibiotics used as medicine.

C. Antibacterial soaps kill a lot of bacteria, and only the hardiest ones survive to reproduce.

D. Antibacterial soaps can be very drying to the skin.

C. Antibacterial soaps kill a lot of bacteria, and only the hardiest ones survive to reproduce.

All of the answer choices in this question are true statements, but the question specifically asks for a cause of increased disease virulence in hospitals. This phenomenon is due to natural selection. The bacteria that can survive contact with antibacterial soap are the strongest ones, and without other bacteria competing for resources, they have more opportunity to flourish. This problem has led to several antibiotic-resistant bacterial diseases in hospitals nationwide. Therefore, the **answer is (C)**. However, note that answers (A) and (D) may be additional problems with over-reliance on antibacterial products.

100. Which of the following is a correct explanation for astronaut 'weightlessness'?

A. Astronauts continue to feel the pull of gravity in space, but they are so far from planets that the force is small.

B. Astronauts continue to feel the pull of gravity in space, but spacecraft have such powerful engines that those forces dominate, reducing effective weight.

C. Astronauts do not feel the pull of gravity in space, because space is a vacuum.

D. Astronauts do not feel the pull of gravity in space, because black hole forces dominate the force field, reducing their masses.

A. Astronauts continue to feel the pull of gravity in space, but they are so far from planets that the force is small.

Gravity acts over tremendous distances in space (theoretically, infinite distance, though certainly at least as far as any astronaut has traveled). However, gravitational force is inversely proportional to distance squared from a massive body. This means that when an astronaut is in space, s/he is far enough from the center of mass of any planet that the gravitational force is very small, and s/he feels 'weightless'. Space is mostly empty (i.e. vacuum), and there are some black holes, and spacecraft do have powerful engines. However, none of these has the effect attributed to it in the incorrect answer choices (B), (C), or (D). The answer to this question must **therefore be (A).**

101. The theory of 'sea floor spreading' explains _____

A. the shapes of the continents.

B. how continents collide.

C. how continents move apart.

D. how continents sink to become part of the ocean floor.

C. How continents move apart.

In the theory of 'sea floor spreading', the movement of the ocean floor causes continents to spread apart from one another. This occurs because crust plates split apart, and new material is added to the plate edges. This process pulls the continents apart, or may create new separations, and is believed to have caused the formation of the Atlantic Ocean. The **answer is (C).**

102. Which of the following animals are most likely to live in a tropical rain forest?

A. Reindeer.

B. Monkeys.

C. Puffins.

D. Bears.

B. Monkeys.

The tropical rain forest biome is hot and humid, and is very fertile—it is thought to contain almost half of the world's species. Reindeer (A), puffins (C), and bears (D), however, are usually found in much colder climates. There are several species of monkeys that thrive in hot, humid climates, so **answer (B) is correct.**

103. Which of the following is *not* a type of volcano?

A. Shield Volcanoes.

B. Composite Volcanoes.

C. Stratus Volcanoes.

D. Cinder Cone Volcanoes.

C. Stratus Volcanoes.

There are three types of volcanoes. Shield volcanoes (A) are associated with non-violent eruptions and repeated lava flow over time. Composite volcanoes (B) are built from both lava flow and layers of ash and cinders. Cinder cone volcanoes (D) are associated with violent eruptions, such that lava is thrown into the air and becomes ash or cinder before falling and accumulating. **'Stratus' (C)** is a type of cloud, not volcano, so it is the correct answer to this question.

104. Which of the following is *not* a property of metalloids?

A. Metalloids are solids at standard temperature and pressure.

B. Metalloids can conduct electricity to a limited extent.

C. Metalloids are found in groups 13 through 17.

D. Metalloids all favor ionic bonding.

D. Metalloids all favor ionic bonding.

Metalloids are substances that have characteristics of both metals and nonmetals, including limited conduction of electricity and solid phase at standard temperature and pressure. Metalloids are found in a 'stair-step' pattern from Boron in group 13 through Astatine in group 17. Some metalloids, e.g. Silicon, favor covalent bonding. Others, e.g. Astatine, can bond ionically. Therefore, **the answer is (D).** Recall that metals/nonmetals/metalloids are not strictly defined by Periodic Table group, so their bonding is unlikely to be consistent with one another.

105. Which of these is a true statement about loamy soil?

A. Loamy soil is gritty and porous.

B. Loamy soil is smooth and a good barrier to water.

C. Loamy soil is hostile to microorganisms.

D. Loamy soil is velvety and clumpy.

D. Loamy soil is velvety and clumpy.

The three classes of soil by texture are: Sandy (gritty and porous), Clay (smooth, greasy, and most impervious to water), and Loamy (velvety, clumpy, and able to hold water and let water flow through). In addition, loamy soils are often the most fertile soils. Therefore, the **answer must be (D)**.

106. Lithification refers to the process by which unconsolidated sediments are transformed into _____

A. metamorphic rocks.

B. sedimentary rocks.

C. igneous rocks.

D. lithium oxide.

B. Sedimentary rocks.

Lithification is the process of sediments coming together to form rocks, i.e. sedimentary rock formation. Metamorphic and igneous rocks are formed via other processes (heat and pressure or volcano, respectively). Lithium oxide shares a word root with 'lithification' but is otherwise unrelated to this question. Therefore, the **answer must be (B)**.

107. Igneous rocks can be classified according to which of the following?

A. Texture.

B. Composition.

C. Formation process.

D. All of the above.

D. All of the above.

Igneous rocks, which form from the crystallization of molten lava, are classified according to many of their characteristics, including texture, composition, and how they were formed. Therefore, **the answer is (D)**.

108. Which of the following is the most accurate definition of a nonrenewable resource?

A. A nonrenewable resource is never replaced once used.

B. A nonrenewable resource is replaced on a timescale that is very long relative to human life-spans.

C. A nonrenewable resource is a resource that can only be manufactured by humans.

D. A nonrenewable resource is a species that has already become extinct.

B. A nonrenewable resource is replaced on a timescale that is very long relative to human life-spans.

Renewable resources are those that are renewed, or replaced, in time for humans to use more of them. Examples include fast-growing plants, animals, or oxygen gas. (Note that while sunlight is often considered a renewable resource, it is actually a nonrenewable but extremely abundant resource.) Nonrenewable resources are those that renew themselves only on very long timescales, usually geologic timescales. Examples include minerals, metals, or fossil fuels. Therefore, the **correct answer is (B)**.

109. The theory of 'continental drift' is supported by which of the following?

A. The way the shapes of South America and Europe fit together.

B. The way the shapes of Europe and Asia fit together.

C. The way the shapes of South America and Africa fit together.

D. The way the shapes of North America and Antarctica fit together.

C. The way the shapes of South America and Africa fit together.

The theory of 'continental drift' states that many years ago, there was one land mass on the earth ('pangea'). This land mass broke apart via earth crust motion, and the continents drifted apart as separate pieces. This is supported by the shapes of South America and Africa, which seem to fit together like puzzle pieces if you look at a globe. Note that answer choices (A), (B), and (D) give either land masses that do not fit together, or those that are still attached to each other. Therefore, the **answer must be (C)**.

110. When water falls to a cave floor and evaporates, it may deposit calcium carbonate. This process leads to the formation of which of the following?

A. Stalactites.

B. Stalagmites.

C. Fault lines.

10. Sedimentary rocks.

B. **Stalagmites**.

To answer this question, recall the trick to remember the kinds of crystals formed in caves. Stalactites have a 'T' in them, because they form hanging from the ceiling (resembling a 'T'). Stalagmites have an 'M' in them, because they make bumps on the floor (resembling an 'M'). Note that fault lines and sedimentary rocks are irrelevant to this question. Therefore, **the answer must be (B)**.

111. A child has type O blood. Her father has type A blood, and her mother has type B blood. What are the genotypes of the father and mother, respectively?

A. AO and BO.

B. AA and AB.

C. OO and BO.

D. AO and BB.

A. **AO and BO.**

Because O blood is recessive, the child must have inherited two O's—one from each of her parents. Since her father has type A blood, his genotype must be AO; likewise her mother's blood must be BO. Therefore, only **answer (A)** can be correct.

112. Which of the following is the best definition for 'meteorite'?

A. A meteorite is a mineral composed of mica and feldspar.

B. A meteorite is material from outer space, that has struck the earth's surface.

C. A meteorite is an element that has properties of both metals and nonmetals.

D. A meteorite is a very small unit of length measurement.

B. A meteorite is material from outer space, that has struck the earth's surface.

Meteoroids are pieces of matter in space, composed of particles of rock and metal. If a meteoroid travels through the earth's atmosphere, friction causes burning and a "shooting star"—i.e. a meteor. If the meteor strikes the earth's surface, it is known as a meterorite. Note that although the suffix –ite often means a mineral, answer (A) is incorrect. Answer (C) refers to a 'metalloid' rather than a 'meteorite', and answer (D) is simply a misleading pun on 'meter'. Therefore, the **answer is (B)**.

113. A white flower is crossed with a red flower. Which of the following is a sign of incomplete dominance?

A. Pink flowers.

B. Red flowers.

C. White flowers.

D. No flowers.

A. Pink flowers.

Incomplete dominance means that neither the red nor the white gene is strong enough to suppress the other. Therefore both are expressed, leading in this case to the formation of pink flowers. Therefore, the **answer is (A)**.

114. What is the source for most of the United States' drinking water?

A. Desalinated ocean water.

B. Surface water (lakes, streams, mountain runoff).

C. Rainfall into municipal reservoirs.

D. Groundwater.

D. Groundwater.

Groundwater currently provides drinking water for 53% of the population of the United States. (Although groundwater is often less polluted than surface water, it can be contaminated and it is very hard to clean once it is polluted. If too much groundwater is used from one area, then the ground may sink or shift, or local salt water may intrude from ocean boundaries.) The other answer choices can be used for drinking water, but they are not the most widely used. Therefore, **the answer is (D)**.

115. Which is the correct sequence of insect development?

A. Egg, pupa, larva, adult.

B. Egg, larva, pupa, adult.

C. Egg, adult, larva, pupa.

D. Pupa, egg, larva, adult.

B. Egg, larva, pupa, adult.

An insect begins as an egg, hatches into a larva (ie. caterpillar), forms a pupa (ie. cocoon), and emerges as an adult (ie. moth). Therefore, the **answer is (B)**.

116. A wrasse (fish) cleans the teeth of other fish by eating away plaque. This is an example of _____ between the fish.

A. parasitism.

B. symbiosis (mutualism).

C. competition.

D. predation.

B. Symbiosis (mutualism).

When both species benefit from their interaction in their habitat, this is called 'symbiosis', or 'mutualism'. In this example, the wrasse benefits from having a source of food, and the other fish benefit by having healthier teeth. Note that 'parasitism' is when one species benefits at the expense of the other, 'competition' is when two species compete with one another for the same habitat or food, and 'predation' is when one species feeds on another. Therefore, the **answer is (B)**.

117. What is the main obstacle to using nuclear fusion for obtaining electricity?

A. Nuclear fusion produces much more pollution than nuclear fission.

B. There is no obstacle; most power plants us nuclear fusion today.

C. Nuclear fusion requires very high temperature and activation energy.

D. The fuel for nuclear fusion is extremely expensive.

C. Nuclear fusion requires very high temperature and activation energy.

Nuclear fission is the usual process for power generation in nuclear power plants. This is carried out by splitting nuclei to release energy. The sun's energy is generated by nuclear fusion, i.e. combination of smaller nuclei into a larger nucleus. Fusion creates much less radioactive waste, but it requires extremely high temperature and activation energy, so it is not yet feasible for electricity generation. Therefore, the **answer is (C)**.

118. Which of the following is a true statement about radiation exposure and air travel?

A. Air travel exposes humans to radiation, but the level is not significant for most people.

B. Air travel exposes humans to so much radiation that it is recommended as a method of cancer treatment.

C. Air travel does not expose humans to radiation.

D. Air travel may or may not expose humans to radiation, but it has not yet been determined.

A. Air travel exposes humans to radiation, but the level is not significant for most people.

Humans are exposed to background radiation from the ground and in the atmosphere, but these levels are not considered hazardous under most circumstances, and these levels have been studied extensively. Air travel does create more exposure to atmospheric radiation, though this is much less than people usually experience through dental X-rays or other medical treatment. People whose jobs or lifestyles include a great deal of air flight may be at increased risk for certain cancers from excessive radiation exposure. Therefore, the **answer is (A)**.

119. Which process(es) result(s) in a haploid chromosome number?

A. Mitosis.

B. Meiosis.

C. Both mitosis and meiosis.

D. Neither mitosis nor meiosis.

B. Meiosis.

Meiosis is the division of sex cells. The resulting chromosome number is half the number of parent cells, i.e. a 'haploid chromosome number'. Mitosis, however, is the division of other cells, in which the chromosome number is the same as the parent cell chromosome number. Therefore, the **answer is (B)**.

120. Which of the following is *not* a member of Kingdom Fungi?

A. Mold.

B. Blue-green algae.

C. Mildew.

D. Mushrooms.

B. Blue-green Algae.

Mold (A), mildew (C), and mushrooms (D) are all types of fungus. Blue-green algae, however, is in Kingdom Monera. Therefore, the **answer is (B)**.

121. Which of the following organisms use spores to reproduce?

A. Fish.

B. Flowering plants.

C. Conifers.

D. Ferns.

D. Ferns.

Ferns, in Division Pterophyta, reproduce with spores and flagellated sperm. Flowering plants reproduce via seeds, and conifers reproduce via seeds protected in cones (e.g. pinecone). Fish, of course, reproduce sexually. Therefore, the **answer is (D)**.

122. What is the main difference between the 'condensation hypothesis' and the 'tidal hypothesis' for the origin of the solar system?

A. The tidal hypothesis can be tested, but the condensation hypothesis cannot.

B. The tidal hypothesis proposes a near collision of two stars pulling on each other, but the condensation hypothesis proposes condensation of rotating clouds of dust and gas.

C. The tidal hypothesis explains how tides began on planets such as Earth, but the condensation hypothesis explains how water vapor became liquid on Earth.

D. The tidal hypothesis is based on Aristotelian physics, but the condensation hypothesis is based on Newtonian mechanics.

B. The tidal hypothesis proposes a near collision of two stars pulling on each other, but the condensation hypothesis proposes condensation of rotating clouds of dust and gas.

Most scientists believe the 'condensation hypothesis,' i.e. that the solar system began when rotating clouds of dust and gas condensed into the sun and planets. A minority opinion is the 'tidal hypothesis,' i.e. that the sun almost collided with a large star. The large star's gravitational field would have then pulled gases out of the sun; these gases are thought to have begun to orbit the sun and condense into planets. Because both of these hypotheses deal with ancient, unrepeatable events, neither can be tested, eliminating answer (A). Note that both 'tidal' and 'condensation' have additional meanings in physics, but those are not relevant here, eliminating answer (C). Both hypotheses are based on best guesses using modern physics, eliminating answer (D). Therefore, the **answer is (B)**.

123. Which of the following units is *not* a measure of distance?

A. AU (astronomical unit).

B. Light year.

C. Parsec.

D. Lunar year.

D. Lunar year.

Although the terminology is sometimes confusing, it is important to remember that a 'light year' (B) refers to the distance that light can travel in a year. Astronomical Units (AU) (A) also measure distance, and one AU is the distance between the sun and the earth. Parsecs (C) also measure distance, and are used in astronomical measurement- they are very large, and are usually used to measure interstellar distances. A lunar year, or any other kind of year for a planet or moon, is the *time* measure of that body's orbit. Therefore, the answer to this **question is (D)**.

124. The salinity of ocean water is closest to _____ .

A. 0.035 %

B. 0.35 %

C. 3.5 %

D. 35 %

C. 3.5 %

Salinity, or concentration of dissolved salt, can be measured in mass ratio (i.e. mass of salt divided by mass of sea water). For Earth's oceans, the salinity is approximately 3.5 %, or 35 parts per thousand. Note that answers (A) and (D) can be eliminated, because (A) is so dilute as to be hardly saline, while (D) is so concentrated that it would not support ocean life. Therefore, the **answer is (C)**.

125. Which of the following will not change in a chemical reaction?

A. Number of moles of products.

B. Atomic number of one of the reactants.

C. Mass (in grams) of one of the reactants.

D. Rate of reaction.

B. Atomic number of one of the reactants.

Atomic number, i.e. the number of protons in a given element, is constant unless involved in a nuclear reaction. Meanwhile, the amounts (measured in moles (A) or in grams(C)) of reactants and products change over the course of a chemical reaction, and the rate of a chemical reaction (D) may change due to internal or external processes. Therefore, the **answer is (B)**.

XAMonline, INC. 21 Orient Ave. Melrose, MA 02176

Toll Free number 800-509-4128

TO ORDER Fax 781-662-9268 OR www.XAMonline.com

MICHIGAN TEST FOR TEACHER EXAMINATION - MTTC - 2007

PO# Store/School:

Address 1:

Address 2 (Ship to other):

City, State Zip

Credit card number_____-_____-_____-_____ expiration_____

EMAIL _____

PHONE   FAX

13# ISBN 2007	TITLE	Qty	Retail	Total
978-1-58197-968-8	MTTC Basic Skills 96			
978-1-58197-954-1	MTTC Biology 17			
978-1-58197-955-8	MTTC Chemistry 18			
978-1-58197-957-2	MTTC Earth-Space Science 20			
978-1-58197-966-4	MTTC Elementary Education 83			
978-1-58197-967-1	MTTC Elementary Education 83 Sample Questions			
978-1-58197-950-3	MTTC English 02			
978-1-58197-961-9	MTTC Family and Consumer Sciences 40			
978-1-58197-959-6	MTTC French Sample Test 23			
978-1-58197-965-7	MTTC Guidance Counselor 51			
978-1-58197-964-0	MTTC Humanities& Fine Arts 53, 54			
978-1-58197-972-5	MTTC Integrated Science (Secondary) 94			
978-1-58197-973-2	MTTC Emotionally Impaired 59			
978-1-58197-953-4	MTTC Learning Disabled 63			
978-1-58197-963-3	MTTC Library Media 48			
978-1-58197-958-9	MTTC Mathematics (Secondary) 22			
978-1-58197-962-6	MTTC Physical Education 44			
978-1-58197-956-5	MTTC Physics Sample Test 19			
978-1-58197-952-7	MTTC Political Science 10			
978-1-58197-951-0	MTTC Reading 05			
978-1-58197-960-2	MTTC Spanish 28			
978-158197-970-1	MTTC Social Studies 84			

	SUBTOTAL	
FOR PRODUCT PRICES GO TO WWW.XAMONLINE.COM	Ship	$8.25
	TOTAL	